HANDBOOK
on
ABORTION

by
Dr. & Mrs. J.C. Willke

i

1st American Edition .... May, 1971

Revised Edition .... June, 1975

Revised Edition .... January, 1979

20th Printing .... January, 1982
Copyright © 1982 Hayes Publishing Co.

Spanish Latin American Edition 1974
Manual Sobre el Aborto, Hiltz & Hayes Pub. Co., Inc.

French Edition 1974
"Le Livre Rouge de L'Avortement" Editions France Empire

Malayan Edition 1974
Bypeen, Kerala, India

Spanish Edition 1975
EUNSA .... Pamplona, Espana

Italian Edition 1978
Movimento per La vita .... Milano

Chinese Edition 1978
Hong Kong

Portuguese Edition 1980
Paulinas—Sao Paulo, Brazil

Swedish Edition 1980
Salt & Light—Jarfalla, Sweden

German Edition 1982

HAYES PUBLISHING CO., INC.
(Formerly Hiltz & Hayes)
Cincinnati, Ohio 45224
phone (513) 681-7559

ii

TABLE OF CONTENTS

FOREWORD

Revised Edition

Now available in many different languages and national editions, HANDBOOK ON ABORTION has become the most widely read book in the world presenting the scientific case for the unborn.

More and more it has become evident that a consistency is noted in the Western world among those who favor abortion. This group begins with a basic social premise that "a woman must have this right." This is the sine-qua-non of the pro-abortion movement. For them, it is basic and beyond challenge, much as a believing Christian starts from "Jesus Christ is God."

Assuming the above to be an absolute unchallengable need, the pro-abortionist must then justify this position. Since the idea of killing humans remains repugnant to most people, this idea has to be denied. Therefore, the cornerstone of their argument has been the denial of the humanity of the being who is killed by abortion. This has partly been accomplished by the semantic gymnastics of words such as "terminate", and "interrupt" pregnancy so that the more accurate biological term "kill" can be avoided. The major ploy however, has been to dehumanize the developing living human in the womb. It is easier to destroy a "fetus", an "embryo", or the "product of conception" than to destory an unborn "baby."

If in fact, the being killed by abortion is not a human life, then, however violent the solution, however damaging it may be to the woman, there is some logic and at times, even seeming compassion to abortion.

If however, the being killed is a human life, a tiny, tiny boy or girl, then every citizen in every nation should be deeply concerned. Then, a bit of study will show that the logic and reasons for the destruction of these weakest, least conscious, smallest and most innocent humans among us by abortion, can be applied just as logically and legally to the weak, only partly conscious, oldest, and most dependent or defective among us by euthanasia. Then truly this is shown to be a civil rights issue of the gravest import.

If your mind is closed, don't bother to read this. If however, you are interested in a short, readable condensation of the world's scientific literature as it pertains to the unborn and to many other answers to the abortion protagonists, then have a look.

Then — make up your mind!

Barbara & Jack Willke

PART 1

HUMAN LIFE?

1

SCHIZOPHRENIC SOCIETY?

The following two items came to your authors' attention within the same week. The one, a confidential letter from the police department of a near-by-city:

> *"Dear Doctor:*
>
> *On Tuesday, November --, 1970, a newborn baby was found in a cardboard box behind a supermarket in our city. Apparently, the baby was born sometime that day, and had been dead eight hours or more when found at 9:30 P.M. The autopsy showed the child had been stabbed seven times, suffered a head concussion, and was strangled with a zipper. In the box was the placenta and the severed umbilical cord. Obviously the baby was born without medical assistance. This may or may not indicate the mother has or will be seeking medical attention as a result thereof. The police request your assistance in locating this woman. . ."*

The other, a newspaper article:

November, 1970

> *"An attempted abortion resulted in the live birth of one of a set of twin babies. Dr. Fritz Fuchs, chief of Obstetrics and Gyne-*

2

cology, New York Cornell Medical Center, explained after being questioned that the saline injection had been successful in killing one fetus but that unexpectedly a second, and live, twin had been delivered. Despite all efforts to save the baby, it died after fifteen hours. Dr. Fuchs noted that in the case of twins it is sometimes impossible to inject the solution into both amniotic sacs."

Why is it that the police are only looking for the woman? What of the doctor?

Didn't the doctor clearly mean to kill both of the twins only one day prior to their birth? Since he succeeded in killing only one, and the other was expelled from his mother's uterus alive, why did he not kill this baby also when he found it yet alive? What magic occurred in his thinking once he saw the baby in daylight compared to when the child still lived in the darkness of his mother's uterus?

Why the total about-face from destruction of life to heroic intensive care attempts at preservation of life?

— — — — — — — — — — — — — —

Three years later the following two items were published in British newspapers during the same week. The first is from THE SUN of July 11, 1974, and was illustrated with a delightful picture of the mother and baby:

"Mother Carol Somers shows off million-to-one baby, Glen, whose miracle birth astonished doctors — and her....For, last October, Mrs. Somers, then ten weeks' pregnant had an abortion. And she was also sterilized as her doctor said it would be dangerous to have more children...Six weeks later, Mrs. Somers, aged 24, returned to the hospital for a check-up — and found that she was still pregnant....She said the amazed woman consultant who performed the

abortion told her: 'It must be the will of God.' Doctors at University College Hospital where Glen was eventually born, said Mrs. Somers may have been expecting twins and only one was aborted....Mrs. Somers was told her unborn baby might have suffered through the sterilization. But she decided to have the child and Glen was born on May 20, a perfect baby boy....Mrs. Somers of Clapton, said: 'We love him with all our hearts and we will never feel that he was unwanted.'"

A mother was diagnosed as having a twin pregnancy of 20 weeks gestation. Amniocentesis revealed one was normal and the other had Down's Syndrome (Mongolism). Dr. T. Kerenyi, at Mt. Sinai Hospital in New York inserted a long needle through the mother's abdominal wall, into the chest of the Down's Syndrome baby, and into its heart. All of the blood (25 ml) was sucked out of the heart, killing the baby.

Twenty weeks later the mother delivered a 2980 gm (6½ lbs) live baby and a 530gm (one pound) shrunken dead baby. The mother did well.

Selective birth in twin pregnancy with discordancy for Down's Syndrome, Kerenyi and Chitkara, Vol. 304, No. 25, pg. 1525, 1981, New England J. Med.

— — — — — — — — — — — —

Let us not judge any of these women, but do let us ask the question again.

What magic occurs:

> at birth in the U.S.A.
> at 28 weeks in England
> at 26 weeks in Maryland (before 1973)
> at 24 weeks in New York (before (1973)
> at 20 weeks in Sweden
> at 16 weeks in Washington (before 1973)
> at 12 weeks in Denmark
> at 10 weeks in France
> — when a "fetus" becomes a "baby"?

Are we a Schizophrenic Society?

2

IS THIS HUMAN LIFE?

Is this human life? This is the question that must first be considered, pondered, discussed, and finally answered. It cannot be brushed aside or ignored. It must be faced and honestly met. Upon its answer hinges the entire abortion question, as all other considerations pale to insignificance when compared with it. In a sense nothing else really matters. If what is growing within the mother is not human life, is just a piece of meat, a glob of protoplasm, then it deserves no respect or consideration at all, and the only valid concern is the mother's physical and mental health, her social well-being, and at times even her convenience.

But if this growing being is a *human* being, then we are in an entirely different situation. If human, he or she must be granted the same dignity and protection of life, health, and well-being that our western civilization has always granted to every other human person. (See Legal Rights, Chapt. 22).

For two millenia in our western culture, written into our Constitutions, specifically protected by our laws, and deeply imprinted into the hearts of all men has existed the absolute value of honoring and protecting the right of each human to live. This has been an unalienable, and unequivocal right. The only exceptions have been that of balancing a life for a life in certain situations or by due process of law.

5

— Never in modern times, except by a small group of physicians in Hitler's Germany and by Stalin in Russia, has a price tag of economic or social usefulness been placed on an individual human life as the price of its continued existence.

— Never in modern times, except by physicians in Hitler's Germany, has a certain physical perfection been required as a condition necessary for the continuation of that life.

— Never since the ancient law of paterfamilias in Rome, has a major nation granted to a father or mother total dominion over the life or death of their child.

— Never in western civilization have we legally allowed innocent humans to be deprived of life without due process of law.

Yet our newly enacted permissive abortion laws do all of the above. They represent a complete about face, a total rejection of one of the core values of western man, and an acceptance of a new ethic in which life has only a relative value. No longer will every human have an absolute right to live simply because he exists. Man will now be allowed to exist only if he measures up to certain standards of independence, physical perfection, or utilitarian usefulness to others. This is a momentous change that strikes at the root of western civilization.

It makes no difference to vaguely assume that human life is more human post-born than pre-born. What is critical is to judge it to be, or not to be, human life. By a measure of "more" or "less" human, one can easily and logically justify infanticide and euthanasia. By the measure of economic and/or social usefulness, the ghastly atrocities of Hitlerian mass murders came to be. One cannot help but be reminded of the anguished comment of a condemned Nazi judge who said to an American judge after the Nuremburg trials: "I never knew it would come to this." The American judge answered simply: *"It came to this the first time you condemned an innocent life."*

Ponder well the words of George Santayana, *"Those who do not remember the past are condemned to relive it."*

The Rise and Fall of the Third Reich.
Wm. Shirer,
Simon & Schuster 1959

Back to our basic question. Is this unborn being, growing within the mother, a human life? Make this judgment with the utmost care, scientific precision, and honesty. Upon it may hinge much of the basic freedom of man in the years to come.

— Judge it to be a mass of cells, a piece of meat? Then vote for abortion-on-demand.

— Judge it to be a human life? Then join us in fighting for his and her right to live, with all the energy and resources at your command.

3

WHEN DOES HUMAN
LIFE BEGIN?

This is the question. Upon its answer all else de-
pendes. A mother who challenged the then existing
laws in Illinois was reported as saying: *"I don't think
it's human. It's too small."*

Perhaps her opinion is as good as that of any
other Mary or Joe we might meet on the street. Many
would agree, many would disagree with her. Our only
observation would be to ask the source of their knowledge upon which both pro and con would base their
opinions.

Pro-abortionists have been mounting a worldwide campaign to effect drastic changes in abortion
laws and practices. Most of the average person's
knowledge has come from a very one-sided presentation of facts, including a number of consistently repeated errors about abortion. It is no surprise that
public opinion is slowly softening in its opposition
to abortion. Few wish to be personally involved in
this messy business, but the siren song of an easy solution seems increasingly acceptable for "others" to
use.

But back to the question:

What is the opinion of natural scientists?

The most distinguished scientific meeting of recent years that considered this question in depth was

the First International Conference on Abortion, held in Washington, D.C., in October 1967. It brought together authorities from around the world in the fields of medicine, law, ethics, and the social sciences. They met together in a "think tank" for several days. The first major question considered by the medical group was, "When does human life begin?"

The medical group was composed of biochemists, professors of obstetrics and gynecology, geneticists, etc., and was represented proportionately as to academic discipline, race, and religion (e.g. 20% were Catholic). Their almost unanimous conclusion (19 to 1) was as follows:

> *"The majority of our group could find no point in time between the union of sperm and egg, or at least the blastocyst stage, and the birth of the infant at which point we could say that this was not a human life."* (Blastocyst stage is shortly after fertilization and would account for twinning.) They continued:

> *"The changes occurring between implantation, a six-weeks embryo, a six months fetus, a one-week-old child, or a mature adult are merely stages of development and matruation."*

There has not been, before nor since, a more important or a more qualified body of natural scientists who, as a group, have thoroughly discussed and come to a conclusion on this subject. Until such time as some other group of equal scientific importance might possibly come to a differing conclusion, we believe that the abortion debate, from a scientific standpoint, must proceed on the assumption that *this is human life.*

What was the basis for their scientific conclusion?

Modern science in the last decade has brought us a spectrum of knowledge about fertilization and early development that we had only guessed at previously in history. We now know that the sperm contributes 50% and that the egg contributes 50% of the new life. The sperm contains the genetic code of the father, and has no life or continuing function beyond the sole goal of its existence, that is, fertilization. The ovum contains the genetic code of the mother and is unquestionably part of her body. It has no other function than to be fertilized, and if it is not, it will die.

When, however, at fertilization, the 23 chromosomes from the sperm join 23 chromosomes from the ovum, a new being is created. Never before in the history of the world nor ever again will a being, identical to this one exist. This is a unique being, genetically totally different from the body of the father or the mother, independent, programmed from within, moving foreward in an ongoing, self-controlled process of maturation, growth, development, and replacement of his or her own dying cells.

This living being, granted a protective environment, is completely independent from the beginning of his or her life at fertilization, and at only ten days of age takes over complete physiologic control of the mother's body, being responsible for stopping his or her mother's menstrual periods.

The ultimate scientific fact that all must face and deal with is that...

> *Nothing, no bits or pieces, will be added*
> *to this living human*
> *being from the time of*
> *fertilization until the*
> *old man dies, nothing*
> *except nutrition.*

Each of us existed in toto at that moment, all that we have done since then is to mature.

But how can it be human at that point? Doesn't it become human later?

Did you "come from" an infant? No. you once

10

were an infant who grew and developed into the child or adult you are today. Nothing has been added to the infant who you once were except nutrition.

Did you "come from" a fertilized ovum? No, you once were a fertilized ovum who grew and developed into the child or adult you are today. Nothing has been added to the fertilized ovum who you once were except nutrition.

You are now more developed, larger, and more mature but you were all there at the beginning.

I've heard the fertilized ovum described as only a blueprint. What of this comparison?

The blueprint of your home is merely the plan for your home. After using this instruction sheet to build your house, you can throw the blueprint away. It has not become the house. The fertilized ovum is not the blueprint but is in fact the house in miniature. It itself will grow into the house in time. It is, in toto, the house already. Your home was built piece by piece and ultimately assumed a shape that could be identified as a house. The tiny human, who you once were, developed into the adult you now are, but you were there totally at conception. All you needed to become the adult you are was nutrition, oxygen, and time.

The lady in the quote above said she didn't think it was human because it was too small. How can it be human when it doesn't look like a human?

If the only scientific instruments you use are your own unaided eyes, then a common judgment that you might make would be that it isn't human until it looks human.

We do have microscopes, ultrasonic stethescopes, and genetic knowledge now that goes far beyond the limited knowledge obtained by your eyes alone. To base your opinion solely on what you see rather than upon what science is capable of telling you isn't very rational. This would apply whether determining if a patient has heart disease or if an unborn fetus is human.

Can't we consider the developing embryo a form of plant or animal life that only becomes human at some later stage of development?

Definitely not! The fertilized seed or ovum of a plant, of an animal, or of a human, upon the moment of fertilization and beginning growth, already is in totality that plant, that animal, or that human. Because of our present scientific knowledge of chromosome and gene structure, and of the intricate genetic programming that we are now aware of, we know that a plant can only develop into what it already is, that is, a plant. An animal, a dog for instalce, can only develop into a dog, and a specific species of that dog. All of this is pre-determined and in totality already exists when fertilization occurs. The same is true of a human.

Why did the scientists say, "at least the blastocyst stage?"

The fertilized ovum is a single cell. Various names are given to subsequent stages of growth. The zygote stage implants in the wall of the uterus, after which we call it a blastocyst. The scientists mentioned this stage so that they could account for the fact that twinning sometimes occurs. Non-identical twins are two separate individuals created by the union of two eggs and two sperm. Identical twins, however, occur when one fertilized ovum or zygote apparently splits into two, after which each of the two divided parts (each now a zygote in itself) grows independently in the very same manner toward full development and maturity as the average single zygote will do. This occurs sometime between fertilization and implantation in the wall of the uterus, but never after implantation.

What of the opinion of the World Medical Association?

"I solemnly pledge myself to consecrate my life to the service of humanity...I will practice my profession with conscience and dignity; the health of my patient will be my first consideration...I will maintain by all means in my power the honour and noble traditions of the medical profession...I will not permit considerations of religion, nationality, race, party politics, or social standing to intervene between my duty and my patient: I will maintain the utmost respect for human life from the time of conception; even under threat, I will not use my medical knowledge contrary to the laws of humanity. I make these promises solemnly, freely, and upon my honour."

Geneva Declaration
World Medical Association
Sept., 1948

Can we say then that one living human being (zygote) can split into two living human beings (identical twins)?

Scientific opinion is far from unanimous about how to consider this. One way of considering it is that the original human zygote, in splitting off a cell of itself or half of itself (whatever exactly happens, we don't know), can be considered in effect the parent of the new human being. This might be a form of parthenogenesis, or non-sexual reproduction. We know that this does occur in certain forms of plant and animal life. We could postulate this type of process to explain identical twinning in a human.

The other possibility is that the existing human being, in splitting, dies, to give new life to two new identicial human beings like himself (herself).

What is crucial to either of these explanations is that, at the time when a total human being exists, he or she should be recognized as such and given all rights due other living human beings.

But what if a person would sincerely doubt that this is human life in the womb?

Even if a person did doubt the presence of actual human life in the uterus at a particular time, what would be the fully human way to go? Perhaps a guide then would be how we have always treated other human life when there has been a doubt that it exists. Would we not resolve a doubt in favor of life? We do not bury those who are doubtfully dead. We would work frantically to help rescue entombed miners, a child lost in the mountains, or a person under a collapsed building. Does a hunter shoot until he knows that it is a deer and not another man? We would suggest that the truly human thing would be to give life the benefit of the doubt.

4

DEVELOPMENT IN THE UTERUS

Basic to the consideration of whether this life within the mother is human or even when this life becomes human must be the presently known scientific facts of the development within the uterus. Much has been learned in recent years. What are the facts? What do we know?

The sperm has life. The ovum has life. Why is either of these lives any different than when the two join and become a fertilized ovum?

The sperm has life but not an independent life; it shares in the life of the body of the father. The sperm is chromosomally and genetically identified as a cell of the father's body. It has reached the endpoint of its maturation. It cannot reproduce itself. It is destined to fertilize an ovum or to die. It is at the end of the line.

The ovum has life but not an independent life; it shares in the life of the body of the mother. The ovum is chromosomally and genetically identified as a cell of the mother's body. It too has reached the endpoint of its maturation. It cannot reproduce itself. Its destiny? To be fertilized or to die. It too is at the end of the line.

But when sperm and ovum join, there is created at that time a new living being. A being that has never before existed in the history of the world, never again will exist; a being not at the end of the line but at the dawn; a being completely intact and containing within itself (himself, herself) the totality of everything that being will ever be; a being moving forward in an orderly process of growth and maturation; a being destined to live within the mother for 8½ months and for as many as 95 years without.

This living being is dependent upon his or her mother for shelter and food, but in all other respects is a totally new, different, unique, and independent being.

Isn't the fertilized ovum only a potential human being?

No. It is not a potential human being. It is, rather, a human being with vast potential. One could say that the sperm and ovum, before their union, constitute a potential human being. Once their union is completed however "they" have become an actual human being.

What if it dies soon after fertilization. Was it human then?

Human death can occur at any time during our journey through life. This could be minutes after fertilization or 95 years after fertilization. Human death is merely the end of human life.

There are some who claim that as many as 30% of fertilized ova are lost in the first week. If this is so, it would mean that there is a mortality rate of 30% in the first week of life. This is not relevant to the question of whether or not this is human life — any more than infant mortality is a justification for infanticide, or death in old age for enthanasia, or the death toll on the roads an argument in favor of capital punishment.

When and where does fertilization occur?

Sperm enter the mother's vagina, swim through

the cavity of her uterus, and out through her Fallopian tubes. The egg, breaking out of the shell of her ovary, is penetrated by one of the sperm. This then becomes a fertilized ovum.

What happens after fertilization?

The fertilized ovum travels slowly back through the Fallopian tube and in approximately one week implants within the nutrient wall of the inside of the uterus.

How many weeks are there in a pregnancy and how do you measure them?

We measure a pregnancy from the time the ovum begins to grow, that is, at the start of a woman's menstrual period. After about two weeks of growth it is released from the ovary. The fertilization of the egg can then occur. This is two weeks before her next period is due. Four of the forty weeks have already elapsed at the time she misses her first period.

But the embryo is just a simple fish-like creature.

"The body of the unborn baby is more complex than ours. Before he is born, the baby has several extra parts to his body which he needs only so long as he lives inside his mother. He has his own space capsule, the amniotic sac. He has his own lifeline, the umbilical cord, and he has his own root system, the placenta. These all belong to the baby himself, not to his mother. They are all developed from his original cell."

THE SECRET WORLD OF A BABY,
Day & Liley, 1968, Random House.

When does the unborn baby's heart begin to beat?

The heartbeat begins between the eighteenth to twenty-fifth day.

James M. Tanner, Gordon Rattray Taylor, and the Editors of Time-Life Books, Growth, New York, Life Science Library, 1965, p. 64.

Ultrasound scanners can pick up the heart action at seven weeks.

T. Schawker, Ultrasound Pictures first-trimester Fetus, Medical World News, p. 50, Feb. 6, 1978

Ultrasonic stethoscopes, now common in Obstetricians' offices allow the mother to actually hear her baby's heart beat as early as eight weeks. An eight week heartbeat tape is available (see Resources, page 202).

When does the brain begin functioning?

Electrical brain waves (electroencephalograph) have been recorded as early as forty days.

H. Hamlin, Life or Death by E.E.G. J.A.M.A., Oct. 12, 1964

The brain itself is completely present by eight weeks. The famous Arnold Gesell has said, *"The organization of his psychosomatic self is well underway"* (at 12 weeks or 3 months).

The scientist measures the definitive end of human life by the end of human brain function as measured on the E.E.G. Why not also then use the onset of that same function as measured on that same instrument as the latest time that a scientist would say that human life begins!

When does the baby quicken?

This is an old English word. Originally, more primitive people thought that there was no life in the womb until the mother felt the "stirring of life." We still speak of the mother "feeling life." This first awareness of movement by the mother, or when she "felt her baby kick" was called "quickening." To assume that the baby wasn't alive and thus not human until "life" was felt was a logical enough conclusion at the time.

We now know that the mother doesn't feel movement until the baby weighs about one pound and is a foot long. Only then is the baby strong enough to kick her hard enough for her to feel it. This is a measure of movement, but a very crude one. Modern research has shown us that quickening or movement actually first occurs at six weeks.

Hooker, Davenport,
THE PRENATAL ORIGIN OF BEHAVIOR,
Univ. of Kansas Press, 1952

"In the sixth to seventh weeks . . . If the area of the lips is gently stroked, the child responds by bending the upper body to one side and making a quick backward motion with his arms. This is called a 'total pattern response' because it involves most of the body, rather than a local part."

Leslie B. Arey, DEVELOPMENTAL ANATOMY,
6th ed., Philadelphia, W.B. Sanders Co., 1954

At eight weeks, if we tickle the baby's nose, he will flex his head backwards away from the stimulus.

A. Hellegers, M.D., FETAL DEVELOPMENT, 31,
Theological Studies, 3, 7, 1970, p. 26.

When do other movements begin?

At nine to ten weeks he squints, swallows, moves his tongue, and if you stroke his palm will make a tight fist.

At eleven to twelve weeks, (3 months) he is sucking his thumb vigorously. (Dr. A. Hellegers, above) The most dramatic accounting of movement very early has been the following:

"Eleven years ago, while giving an anesthetic for a ruptured tubal pregnancy (at two months), I was handed what I believed to be the smallest human being ever seen. The em-

19

bryo sac was intact and transparent. Within the sac was a tiny (one-third inch) human male swimming extremely vigorously in the amniotic fluid, while attached to the wall by the umbilical cord. This tiny human was perfectly developed with long, tapering fingers, feet and toes. It was almost transparent as regards the skin, and the delicate arteries and veins were prominent to the ends of the fingers.

"The baby was extremely alive and swam about the sac approximately one time per second with a natural swimmers stroke. This tiny human did not look at all like the photos and drawings of 'embryos' which I have seen, nor did it look like the few embryos I have been able to observe since then, obviously because this one was alive.

"When the sac was opened, the tiny human immediately lost its life and took on the appearance of what is accepted as the appearance of an embryo at this stage (blunt extremeties, etc.)."

Paul E. Rockwell, M.D., Director of Anesthesiology,
Leonard Hospital, Troy, New York
U.S. Supreme Ct., Markle v. Abele, 72-56, 72-730, p. 11

When does he start to breathe?

By eleven to twelve weeks, (3 months) he is breathing fluid steadily and continues so until birth. At birth, he will breathe air. He does not drown by breathing fluid within his mother, because he obtains his oxygen from his umbilical cord. This does, however, develop the organs of respiration.

LIFE BEFORE BIRTH, Life Magazine reprint, p. 13, 1965

Maternal cigarette smoking during pregnancy decreases the frequency of fetal breathing by 20%. The "well documented" higher incidence of pre-

20

maturity, stillbirth, and slower development of reading skill may be related to this decrease.

F. Manning, Meeting Royal Col. Phy & Surg. Canada, Family Practice News, 3-15-76

The measurement of fetal breathing movements may soon provide an indication of fetal well being that is at least as useful as the evaluation of the fetal heart rate.

In the 11th week of gestation fetal breathing is irregular and episodic. As gestation continues, the breathing movements become more vigorous and rapid.

G. Dawes, Ibid above

What of his stomach?

His stomach secretes gastric juice by eight weeks.

What of detailed development like fingernails and eyelashes?

Fingernails are present by eleven to twelve weeks; eyelashes by sixteen.

When would you say all his body systems are present?

By eight weeks. (2 months)

At what point are all his body systems working?

By eleven weeks.

LIFE BEFORE BIRTH reprint.

How about teeth?

All twenty milk-teeth buds are present at six-and-a-half weeks.

LIFE BEFORE BIRTH reprint.

Can an unborn baby cry?

"At eighteen weeks, (4 months) equipped with a

full set of vocal cords, it can go through the motions of crying but without air cannot make a sound."

LIFE BEFORE BIRTH, reprint, p. 16

Certain experiments with unborn babies still in the womb have involved replacing some of the fluid with air so as to outline the baby's movements and position on X-ray photographs. Some of the baby's positions were such that when the mother laid on her back, the little nose and mouth extended into the air bubble. The baby breathed out the fluid in his lungs and breathed in the air. Some of the older stronger babies cried loud enough to keep their mothers awake that night and loud enough to be heard by others. When the mother would roll on her side, she would submerge the nose and mouth under water again. The baby would breathe out the air, breathe back in the fluid and the sound would stop.

A. William Liley — Professor — OB & GYN,
University of Auckland, New Zealand

How does the size of the baby increase in weight?

At twelve weeks (3 months) he weighs one ounce, at sixteen weeks six ounces, and at twenty weeks (4 months) approximately one pound.

Why do so many legal documents speak of twenty weeks survival time?

This is again an obsolete concept which should be discarded. Dr. James Diamond has said that this *"twenty week survival time is about as sacred as the four-minute mile."*

AMERICA, July 19, 1969, p. 37

A full term pregnancy lasts 40 weeks or 9 months. Viability thirty years ago was at 30 weeks. Today it is as low as 20 weeks (see fig. I). By the turn of the century it will be down to 10 or 12 weeks and with artificial placentae, earlier than that.

It should be obvious that the babies haven't changed. What has changed has been the sophistication of the external life support systems around the baby. To measure humanity or the baby's right to life by viability is completely irrational. Viability does not measure the baby but rather the scientific sophistication and equipment of those around the baby.

But some laws held abortion legal until the baby is "viable." What does this mean?

Most people define viable as "capable of independent existence." We believe this should be stricken from the law books. By this definition, even a seven-pound baby after birth is not viable. Leave this healthy full-term child alone and he will die in a few days from neglect. He is not capable of independent existence, but depends totally on the life support given him by his mother.

When is a child capable of independent existence?

Certainly not before he's old enough to go to school. And we can make a pretty good case for him not being capable of it much before he's a teenager.

How early can a baby survive?

Your authors have thoroughly documented babies who were born to survive at the following ages as dated from first day of last normal menstrual period.

Two babies at 25 weeks, two at 24, one at 23, one at 22, two at 21, and one at 20 weeks.

Are they normal?

All of these are. Many still think otherwise. This is probably a holdover from the days before intensive neonatal care units. It is now documented that babies born, weighing under 1,000 grams (2.2 lbs.) now survive 30-40% of the time and with "normal functions and minimal neurologic defect."

The expense of such care compares with coronary bypass surgery which only extends life a few years at best compared to the entire lifetime granted to such a surviving child.

Dr. Pomerance, U. of Cal. at L.A., Med. World News,
Oct. 3, 1977

What does legal "viability" mean as far as legal rights of the unborn child are concerned?

Some have used "viability" as a measure of judgment as to whether or not the unborn child has the basic human right to protection of his life by the state. The frightening aspect of using this as a dimension of right to life is quickly apparent when we consider that, by this standard, a defective newborn child or a defective child of any age is also not "viable". By the above criteria, the senile old person rendered incompetent by a stroke, the completely psychotic individual, or even the quadraplegic war veterans are all not "viable", as they are not capable of independent existence. Some of the above also do not have mental "viability." To make a judgment of an unborn child's right to live or not in our society by this mental or physical competence, rather than merely by the fact that he is human and alive, bring only too close the state's determination of a person's right to continued life as measured by their mental or physical competence or whatever the current price tag is.

What measure would you use instead of viability?

We would ask:

a) Is this being alive?

Yes. He has the characteristics of life. That is, he can reproduce his own cells and develop them into a specific pattern of maturity and function.

b) Is this being human?

Yes. This a unique being, distinguishable totally from any other living organism, completely human in all of his characteristics, including the human forty-six chromosomal pattern, and can develop only into a fully mature human.

c) Is this being complete?

Yes. Nothing new will be added from the time of union of sperm and egg until the death of the old man except growth and development of what is already there at the beginning. All he needs is time to develop and mature.

What is birth?

Birth is the emergence of the infant from the mother's womb, the severing of the umbilical cord, and the beginning of the child's existence physically detached from the mother's body. The only change that occurs at birth is a change in the external life support system of the child. The child is no different before birth than after, except that he has changed his method of feeding and obtaining oxygen. Before birth, nutrition and oxygen were obtained from the mother through the baby's umbilical cord. After birth, oxygen is obtained from his own lungs and nutrition through his own stomach, if he is mature enough to be nourished that way. If he is quite premature, nourishment would continue through our present reasonably sophisticated external life support systems in the form of intravenous feedings, which is similar to the umbilical cord feeding from the mother.

What of a cell from some part of a person's body that can be kept alive in a tissue culture, either separated from his living body or maintained after that person has died. Does this not upset the concept of the fertilized ovum as a human life?

No. Those cells were a part of a person and can only reproduce themselves as a specific type of cell. The fertilized ovum is not a part of another person but is a whole person itself. It will not merely reproduce itself but is in totality a complete human be-

25

ing and will grow into a full adult if given time. Any one of hundreds of millions or billions of these cells in a human person's body can die and we do not say that the person has died. When a single fertilized ovum cell, however, dies, the entire new person is dead.

The other important difference is that the fertilized ovum, subdividing and multiplying into many cells, moves immediately in the direction of specialized and differing parts, which are organized in a single unified complex being. Cells from parts of an adult human body in tissue culture can only reproduce their own kind and cannot go on to develop differing specialized parts.

Does Dr. Liley, the "Father of Fetology," think he (it) is human?

Dr. Liley, who developed fetal blood transfusion, has said that seven days after fertilization *"the young individual, in command of his environment and destiny with a tenacious purpose, implants in the spongy lining and with a display of physiological power suppresses his mother's menstrual period. This is his home for the next 270 days and to make it habitable the embryo develops a placenta and a protective capsule of fluid for himself. He also solves, single-handed, the homograft problem, that dazzling feat by which foetus and mother, although immunological foreigners who could not exchange skin grafts nor safely receive blood from each other, nevertheless tolerate each other in parabiosis for nine months."*

"We know that he moves with a delightful easy grace in his buoyant world, that foetal comfort determines foetal position. He is responsive to pain and touch and cold and sound and light. He drinks his amniotic fluid, more if it is artificially sweetened, less if it·is given an unpleasant taste. He gets hiccups and sucks his thumb. He wakes and sleeps. He gets bored with repetitive signals but can be taught to be alerted by a first signal for a second different one. And finally

he determines his birthday, for unquestionably the onset of labour is a unilateral decision of the foetus."

"This then is the foetus we know and indeed we each once were. This is the foetus we look after in modern obstetrics, the same baby we are caring for before and after birth, who before birth can be ill and need diagnosis and treatment just like any other patient."

Liberal Studies, "A CASE AGAINST ABORTION,"
Whitcombe & Tombs, Ltd., 1971.

Wouldn't a successful human clone upset this reasoning?

First, there has never been a human clone. It may well be that man, the highest species, can never be successfully cloned. However, even granting that possibility, the clone, at the first moment of his existence, would be a fully human life. He or she would be, in effect, the identical twin of the donor human, but of a different age. Being a total human, this person would in justice, be due the same equal protection of the law as the older donor human.

Is Growth a Continuous Process?

Yes, from the time of fertilization. There are a total of 45 generations of doubling of the number of cells during the life of the human body. The first two for one division occurs right after fertilization. Seven more are completed by the time of implantation (about 7 days old). By eight weeks of life, a total of 30 doublings occurred, and by 28 weeks, 39 doublings. At birth, 41 have been completed but it takes another 15-20 years for the final four divisions. After adult size is reached (45 divisions) all that happens is replacement of dying cells as no new growth occurs.

It is a scientific fact that the human body has completed 90% of his or her growth at the time of birth. Only 10% occurs between birth and adulthood. None after that.

The Tiniest Humans, A.W. Liley, pg. 14,
Sassone Pub., California

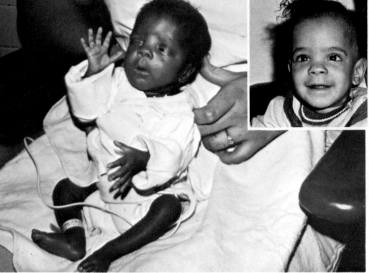

Fig. I. Baby Marcus Richardson, born 1-1-72 at Cincinnati General Hospital exactly 20 weeks (4½ months) from the first day of his mother's last menstrual period. An entirely normal child, he is shown 10 weeks after birth and 10 months after birth.

Fig. II. Eleven weeks old, almost 3 months. All organ systems now function

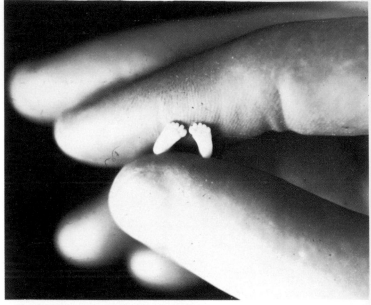

Fig. III. Tiny human feet at ten weeks, perfectly formed.

Fig. IV. This tiny human was yet alive at this moment, only 6 weeks after first day of last menstrual period, a just removed tubal pregnancy.
(Photo by Robert Wolfe, with permission Bell Museum of Pathology, University of Minnesota.)

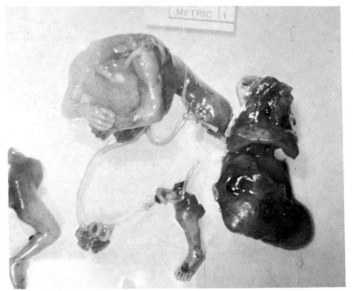

Fig. V. by Scraping

Fig. VI. by Suction at 10 weeks

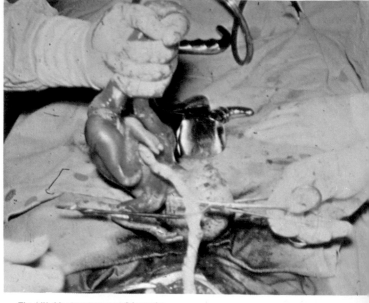

Fig. VII. Hysterotomy at 24 weeks

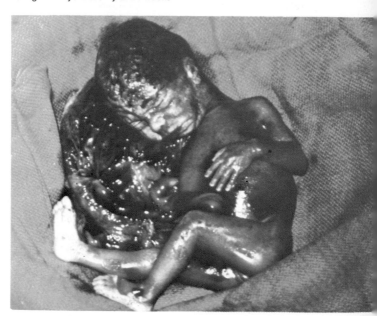

Fig. VIII. Salt Poisoning at 19 weeks

5

HOW ABORTIONS
ARE DONE

There are five methods commonly used in performing an abortion. Nature has a sixth way, commonly called a miscarriage.

What is a miscarriage?

A miscarriage or "spontaneous abortion" happens when the uterus, for natural reasons, goes into labor early in pregnancy.

Why does this happen?

We don't always know. Usually the growing baby has died because of abnormalities of itself or its placenta, and after this has occurred, the mother has the miscarriage.

Is this dangerous?

Most miscarriages could quite safely occur at home. There is sometimes excessive bleeding, however, or incomplete emptying of the uterus requiring hospitalization. Even when a D&C is needed there is rarely damage to the mother as the cervix (womb opening) softens and opens itself. The surgeon then gently teases the rotting remnants of the placenta, (afterbirth) from the inside walls with a blunt instrument. Infection is rare. Baby parts are seldom found.

What are the five kinds of induced abortion?

They are: 1) Suction aspiration, 2) Dilatation and curretage and D & E, 3) Prostaglandin, 4) Salt Poisoning, and 5) Hysterotomy. (See Fig. V, VI, VII, VIII).

What is the Suction Method?

To use this method the surgeon must first paralyze the cervical muscle ring (womb opening), then stretch it open. This is difficult because it is hard or "green" and not ready to open. He then inserts a hollow plastic tube with a knife-like edge on the tip, into the uterus. The suction tears the baby into pieces. He then cuts the deeply rooted placenta from the inner wall of the uterus. The scraps are sucked out into a bottle, (see Fig. VI). The suction is 29 times more powerful than a home vacuum cleaner.

What is a "D & C"?

This is similar to the suction type except that he inserts a curette, a loop shaped steel knife, up into the uterus. With this he cuts the placenta and baby into pieces and scrapes them out into a basin. Bleeding is usually profuse. (Fig. V)

The suction is the safest way, isn't it?

Many enthusiasts are loudly saying so, but all surgeons don't agree. Profuse hemorrhage is common in the first few days after this method is used. When this happens a second "D & C" with instruments must be done and often blood transfusions are needed. Neither suction nor D & C should be used after 12 weeks (3 months).

What is a D & E?

This is a D & C done after 12 weeks. This method has always been regarded as extremely dangerous to the mother. A report from the Center for Disease Control, Dept. HEW, states however, that it is still safer than salt poisoning or Prostaglandin use.

Comparative Risks of Three Methods of
Midtrimester Abortion, Morbidity and Mortality
Weekly Report. November 26, 1976

What about the small catheter (Karman) and the menstrual extraction type?

These are true suction abortions but more frequently leave parts in the uterus. Because of this infection and hemorrhage are common.

What is a Prostaglandin Abortion?

These are drugs recently developed by the Upjohn Co. of Kalamazoo. Prostin E2 Suppositories, F2 Alpha or Prostion F-15 in shot form, when they work, will produce labor and delivery at whatever stage of pregnancy a woman is. If the baby is old enough to survive the trauma of labor, it will usually be born alive, but usually too small to survive. Of course, the entire purpose of an abortion is to kill the baby so, to have one born alive, is considered a "complication."

Upjohn is the first major drug company that has abandoned the ethic of producing only drugs that will save lives and is now making one, the specific purpose of which is to kill. For this reason many pro-life people have stopped using its products since they do not want to support such a company.

Are the Prostaglandins Safe?

". . . a large complication rate (42.6%) is associated with its use. Few risks in obstetrics are more certain than that which occurs to a pregnant woman undergoing abortion after the 14th week of pregnancy."

Complications following Prostaglandin F-2 Alpha
induced mid-trimester abortion
Duenhoelter & Grant, J. OB & GYN, Sept. 1975

What is the saline or salt poisoning method?

This is done after the 16th week. A large needle is inserted through the abdominal wall of the mother and into the baby's amniotic sac. A concentrated salt solution is injected into the amniotic fluid. The baby breathes and swallows it, is poisoned, struggles, and sometimes convulses. It takes over an hour to kill the baby. When successful, the mother goes into labor about one day later and delivers a dead baby. Any nurse in an aborting hospital can tell of a significant number of these babies who are born still alive. (Fig. VIII)

Some doctors refer to salt poisoned babies as "candy apple babies", why is this?

The corrosive effect of the concentrated salt, often burns and strips away the entire outer layer of the baby's skin. This exposes the raw, red, glazed looking subcutaneous layer. The baby's head sometimes looks like a "candy apple."

Is it actually poisoning?

Yes, the mechanism of death is of acute hypernatremia or acute salt poisoning, with development of widespread vasodilitation, edema, congestion, hemorrhage, shock and death.

Fetal Pathology and Mechanism of Death in
Saline Abortion, Galen et al Am. J. OB & GYN,
120: 347-355, 1974.

What is a hysterotomy?

This is like a Caesarian section. The mother's abdomen is surgically opened, as is her uterus. The baby is then lifted out, and, with the placenta, discarded (see Fig. VII). This method is usually used late in pregnancy. One surgeon in our area who used this method removed a tiny baby who breathed, tried to cry, and was moving his arms and legs — so he threw the placenta on top of the baby and smothered him.

How large are some aborted babies?

"Responsible" physicians would hope not to abort a mother whose baby would be over one pound. But — one of our colleagues recently witnessed a four pound baby killed by the salt method and delivered stillborn. Another practice of some so-called physicians in New York and elsewhere is that of injecting salt solution and immediately sending the mother home. Within two weeks in Cincinnati two babies weighing three-and-a-fourth and three-and-three-fourths pounds, were delivered dead from mothers who had had this procedure. We find it hard not to call this, by any standard, deliberate murder.

Are babies ever born alive from abortions?

Almost all babies aborted by hysterotomy are born alive. If they are large enough many Prostaglandin babies are born alive. Occasionally, salt poisoning abortions also deliver live babies.

They must then either be killed or left to die from lack of attention.

— One baby in New York that was "aborted" in this manner refused to die and has been adopted.

U.P.I., Dec. 19, 1970

— In California, a 4 pound baby was born alive after a salt injection. As reported, the doctor ordered the nurse not to use oxygen to save the baby. She replied that if she did not, it would die. The doctor replied, "wasn't that the original idea?" — She gave oxygen anyway. The baby lived and has been adopted.

The Bakersfield Californian,
BABY DEATH TRY LAID TO PHYSICIAN,
Sept. 25, 1973.

— Dr. Christopher Tietse, in reporting on 73,000 abortions lists hysterotomies as 1.3% of the total. Almost all hysterotomy babies are born alive. If we use a 1971 New York total to be close to 300,000 abortions (higher than official figures since a large percentage are not reported) it is evident that 3,900 babies, aborted by hysterotomy, were born alive and allowed to (or encouraged to) die. This contrasts sharply with the published figures of 40 to 60.

— The "Stobhill Hospital baby" in Glasgow was aborted by this technique. This child·was carried from the operating theatre in a paper disposal bag, and left in the snow outside the porter's lodge for about 30 mintues until the porter picked it up to throw it into the incinerator. He was about to do so when he heard the baby cry. He rushed it back to the operating theatre where it was resuscitated and despite bad head injuries survived for hours. Subsequently a public inquiry was carried out — but no action could be brought against those involved because they had been acting "legally."

At the public inquiry on this baby the Procurator Fiscal (or Coroner) suggested that a baby aborted "alive" should be resuscitated. The Pathologist to whom he addressed the remark replied that "this would defeat the purpose of the Abortion Act." The purpose of the English Abortion Law is to ensure that these children do not survive.

— In the famous Waddel case in California in 1978, a survivor of salt poisoning, a nearly full term baby girl, was, according to the Coroner's report, killed by manual strangulation.

Is surgery on an ectopic Pregnancy an Abortion?

No, not at least in the usual way we consider abortion. By the time most ectopic surgery is done, the developing baby is dead and often destroyed by the hemorrhage. In any case, surgery is done primarily to prevent the death of the mother and is good medical practice as there is no chance for a surviving baby.

How about removal of a cancerous pregnant uterus?

The same applies. Surgery is done to prevent the death of the mother. The death of the baby is an unfortunate and undesired secondary effect. If at all possible, the baby would be saved.

What about the direct abortion to prevent the death of the mother?

This would be a true "therapeutic" abortion, and is almost non-existent today. If the mother's actual life were threatened, a conscientious doctor would try to save both. In the rare, rare case where such a decision really needed to be made, the problem would be that of balancing one human life against another, (note that all other reasons given for abortion are reasons less than human life itself).

In such a case, it would be proper to give to the local family, and local medical and ethical authorities the right to make whatever decision that they feel is right.

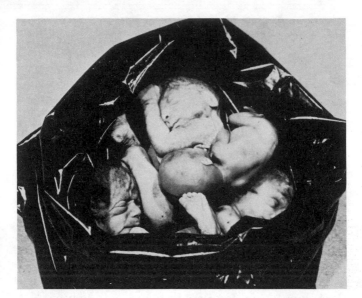

Fig. IX. This was the result of one morning's work in a Canadian teaching hospital.

These babies had attained fetal ages of from 18-24 weeks (4-5 months) before being killed by abortion.

PART II

PRICE TAG:

A NEW ETHIC?

ABORTION AND PUBLIC OPINION

There have been a number of public opinion polls in recent years. Many of these results seem to point to a slow change of opinion toward favoring abortion.

There have been two major recent polls which, by their sheer size, have reduced to insignificance all previous ones. The citizens of the states of North Dakota and Michigan went to the polls in November 1972 to cast their votes on proposals to adopt abortion-on-demand until 20 weeks.

The pro-abortion forces had carefully chosen both states. North Dakota was only 12% Catholic. Michigan, a polygot state, had 51% of its people unchurched and all polls there showed that over 60% were pro-abortion.

The major newspapers, especially in Michigan, mounted a heavy pro-abortion propaganda campaign. The pro-abortion forces, heavily funded, purchased numerous full page ads and TV and radio shorts. Some radio and TV stations were heavily pro-abortion while others did allow equal time to both sides. Lacking such control or such funds, the pro-life advocates used their chief resource, volunteer people, deeply concerned people. They conducted their educative campaign door-to-door through both states.

By election day a saturation educational effort had been conducted by both sides. This was a first in recent history.

The results? Michigan voted no on abortion by 62%. North Dakota voted no on abortion by 78%.

Two months later this overwhelming expression of the wishes of the citizens of the United States was totally ignored and their mandate nullified by the decision of seven Supreme Court Justices.

A NEW ETHIC?

But aren't we seeing a new ethic develop as to the value of human life?

Some are trying to say so. It might be interesting to quote a recent editorial:

> "*The reverence of each and every human life has been a keystone of western medicine, and is the ethic which has caused physicians to try to preserve, protect, repair, prolong, and enhance every human life.*
>
> "*Since the old ethic has not yet been fully displaced, it has been necessary to separate the idea of abortion from the idea of killing which continues to be socially abhorrent. The result has been a curious avoidance of the scientific fact, which everyone really knows, that human life begins at conception, and is continuous, whether intra- or extra-uterine, until death. The very considerable semantic gymnastics which are required to rationalize abortion as anything but taking a human life would be ludicrous if they were not often put forth under socially impeccable auspices. It is suggested that this schizophrenic sort of subterfuge is necessary because, while a new ethic is being accepted, the old one has not yet been rejected.*"

JOURNAL, California State Medical Assn., Sept. 1970

6

RAPE, INCEST

Picture the poor helpless girl, possibly your daughter, assaulted by an unknown assailant, frightened, tearful, emotionally upset. Then a few weeks later, confirmation of her worst fears — she's pregnant.

Who would be so heartless and so cruel as to refuse her an abortion? Why must this innocent girl be forced through the ordeal of pregnancy and childbirth? Talk is easy, as long as this is theoretical, but what if this were your daughter?

The above situation, charged as it is with emotionalism, pathos, and sympathy, has been sufficient to convince some legislators to enact laws that permit abortion for rape or for incest. Is there anything more that can be said?

Is pregnancy from assault rape very common?

No. It is extremely rare.

Can you prove this?

A study of one thousand rape victims who were treated medically right after the rape reported no pregnancies.

L. Kuchera, Postcoital Contraception with Diethylstilbesterol, JAMA, Oct. 25, 1971

Why?

We do not know. Obviously, many women (and

men) are infertile for a variety of reasons. Also, a study has shown that 58% of assaultants were "sexually dis-functional" at the time.

Sexual Medicine Today, Jan. 1978, p. 16.

Perhaps there is tubal spasm, some negative female hormone effect or other reasons.

How many assault rape pregnancies are there?

In 1977, in the U.S., there were 63,020 forcible rapes. As there are about 100,000,000 females in the country old enough to be at risk. This means that one in 1,600 per year is raped.

If we use a very high figure and calculate on the basis of one pregnancy in 1,000 forcible rapes, (there are probably far fewer pregnancies) we find only 63 pregnancies per year in the entire nation or one a year in a state of 3½ million people.

Are there any statistics to support the fact that pregnancy is rare?

There have been few good statistical studies in this country. In Czechoslovakia, however, out of 86,000 consecutive induced abortions, only twenty-two were done for rape. At a recent obstetric meeting at a major midwest hospital, a poll taken of those physicians present (who had delivered over 19,000 babies) revealed that not one had delivered a bona fide rape pregnancy.

What has been the English experience?

In 1938, Dr. Aleck Bourne had a fourteen-year-old girl brought to him who had been raped. She was in severe shock. He did the abortion, and then gave him-self up to the police. He was tried and finally ac-quitted on the grounds that he had performed the op-eration in order to save the girl's sanity. It was on the findings of this trial that British law was based until all Abortion was legalized in 1967. For many years it was very conservatively interpreted to provide protection for doctors to use their medical judgment in "the hard cases." Ultimately, however it opened the door to abortion on demand.

It is significant to point out that this same Aleck Bourne, "appalled" by the way in which the results of his trial ultimately opened the door to abortion-on-demand and all of its abuses, became a founding member of the Society for the Protection of Unborn Children in 1967.

What is meant by "difficulty of proving rape"?

This is the crux of the problem and it goes something like this: Let's assume a young woman is raped, but that through fright or ignorance she does not report it and quietly nurses her fears. She misses her period and hopes against hope that it isn't what she thinks it is. Another month, another month, and finally in tears she reports to her mother, her physician, or some other counselor or confidante. To prove rape then is impossible. The only proof of rape, in fact, is either to have a reliable witness corroborate the story, or to have her come immediately for help after the incident.

What of incest?

Incest is intercourse by a father with his daughter, uncle with niece, etc. The same dynamics mentioned above apply. Will Uncle John admit to having relations with his niece? Never! It would be her word against his. The court might even believe her, but could not act on it legally. Incestuous intercourse is seldom reported and when pregnancy does occur, it is not usually reported as being from incest.

What of a law for rape or incest then?

We would call them non-laws, as they would be almost totally inoperative. We believe that rape and incest as reasons for legalizing abortion laws are little but an emotional smoke screen behind which to open the door for permissive abortion for many other reasons.

But, even if rare, some girls are forcefully raped and some do get pregnant. Should they be forced to carry an unwanted child?

Legal authorities say that to change the entire law for a few rare cases would open a Pandora's Box.

Responsible lawmakers have always agreed that "hard cases make bad laws." This means that laws must speak to the general norm. Judges have always allowed certain exceptions to laws or to punishment out of mercy for a "hard" or tragic case. The Bourne Case was a good example until some judges and countries (like Jamaica) stretched its meaning to allow abortion-on-demand.

To our knowledge, no physician has been prosecuted in recent times in the U.S. or Canada for doing an abortion in such a case even though the law forbade it.

But many wouldn't even allow it for rape?

Unquestionably, many would want her to destroy the growing baby within her. But before making this decision, remember that most of the trauma has already occurred. She has been raped. That trauma will live with her all of her life. Furthermore, this girl did not report for help but kept this to herself. For several weeks or months she has thought of little else. Now she has finally asked for help, has shared her upset, and should be in a supportive situation.

The utilitarian question from the mother's standpoint is whether or not it would now be better to kill the developing baby within her. But will abortion now be best for her, or will it bring her more harm yet? What has happened and its damage has already occurred. She's old enough to know and have an opinion as to whether she carries a "baby" or a "blob of protoplasm."

Will she be able to live comfortably with the memory that she killed her developing baby? Or would she ultimately be more mature and more at peace with herself if she could remember that, even though she was unwillingly pregnant, she nevertheless solved her problem by being unselfish, by giving of herself and of her love to an innocent baby who had not asked to be created, to deliver, perhaps to adopt if she decides that is what is best for her baby.

Compare this memory with the woman who can only look back and say "I killed my baby."

Even from only the mother's standpoint, the choice is one which deserves the most serious deliberation, and no answer is easy.

But wouldn't it be safer physically to abort a young girl than to let her deliver?

— Physical and emotional damage from abortion is greater in a young girl. "*Adolescent abortion candidates differ from their sexually mature counterparts, and these differences contribute to higher morbidity.*"
C. Cowell, University of Toronto, Ortho Panel 14

— Prof. J.K. Russel states that girls of school age have extra risks from abortion as they have small tightly closed cervixes which are especially liable to damage on dilatation.

   "*Evidence has accumulated steadily over the past 10 years of increased risks for these young mothers.*"
Russel, G.P. (England) 1-10-1974

— "the younger the patient and the further along she is in her pregnancy, the greater the complication rate."
Deaths And Near Deaths With Legal Abortions, M. Bulfin, meeting Am. Col. OB & GYN, Florida, 1975

43

—"Obstetric and neonatal risks for teenagers over 15 are no greater than for women in their twenties provided they receive adequate care."

E. McAnarney, meeting Society Adolescent Medicine, Family Practice News, Feb. 1978, p. 6

—Pregnancy in a very young teenager (12-16 years) does not appear to be inherently high risk."

J. Durger, Roosevelt Hosp., N.Y., Fam. Practice News, p. 7, May 1, 1978

But in a rape pregnancy, everyone loses!

That is wrong. Once after answering a question on rape on a radio show, one of your authors was called to the phone after the program. A woman's voice said *"You were talking about me. You see I am the product of rape. An intruder forced his way into my parent's house, tied up my father and with him watching, raped my mother. I was conceived that night. Everyone advised an abortion. The local doctors and hospital were willing. My father however, said 'Even though not mine, that is a child and I will not allow it to be killed!'*

I don't know how many times, as I lay secure in the loving arms of my husband, I have thanked God for my wonderful Christian father."

---

for finally:

Isn't is a twisted logic

that would kill an innocent

unborn baby for the crime

of his father!

7

MENTAL HEALTH

— *Of a total of 62,672 hospital abortions performed during 1970, in California, 98.2% were for mental health.*

California Dept. of Public Health
Report to California Legislature

— *New York didn't require the subterfuge of "mental health". It reported only 2% done for this reason.*

— *Dr. Louis Hellman, Deputy Asst. Sect. of HEW, who is strongly pro-abortion, said at Columbia Women's Hospital, Washington, D.C., that the requirement of a psychiatrist's permission for abortion is a "gross sham".*

Washington Post, Nov. 25, 1971.

How new is mental health as an indication for abortion?

It is quite new and has been spoken of only in the last few years. Since the decline and virtual disappearance of therapeutic abortion of the type that once was necessary to save the life of the mother, many major university hospitals have gone a decade or more without doing a single therapeutic abortion. For instance, the University Hospital of the College of Medicine at the University of Cincinnati did not do a single therapeutic abortion for fifteen years prior to 1968. This experience is not unusual.

W. Stone, Dept. of Psychiatry, U. of C., Feb., 1971.

Already in 1951, Dr. R.J. Hefferman, of Tufts University, said: *"Anyone who performs a therapeutic abortion (for physical disease) is either ignorant of modern methods of treating the complications of pregnancy, or is unwilling to take time to use them."*

Congress of American College of Surgeons, 1951

But isn't it sometimes necessary to preserve her mental health?

The word "mental health" is so broad and vague as to be almost meaningless. In fact, in the last few years, it has become a catch-all reason for which all sorts of abortions have been justified, only rarely in fact being done for serious psychiatric reasons. When a country permits abortion for mental health, that country has abortion-on-demand.

What would be a serious psychiatric reason?

Frank Ayd, M.D., medical editor and nationally known psychiatrist has said: *"True psychiatric reasons for abortion have become practically non-existent. Modern psychiatric therapy has made it possible to carry a mentally ill woman to term."*

It can be flatly stated that no mental disease known to man can be cured by abortion. The most that can be said is that possible mental breakdowns or complications might be prevented by abortion. To predict this accurately, however, is quite frankly beyond the competence of ordinary men, and we include psychiatrists in this group. There are so many variables, people are so different, and react in so many different ways, that no one, no matter what his training, can accurately predict what effect a pregnancy or an abortion will have on a woman.

That's one opinion. Can you cite other authorities?

Dr. Theodore Litz, Yale University Psychiatrist, has said: *"It is practically impossible to predict when an abortion will not be more detrimental to the mental health of the mother than carrying her child to birth."*

Dr. R. Bruce Sloan of Temple University (who would permit abortions), writing in the New England Journal of Medicine, May 29, 1969, said: *"There are no unequivocable psychiatric indications for abortions."* He stated further that if the pregnancy is not interrupted. *"The risk of flare-up or precipitation of psychosis is small and unpredictable, and suicide is rare."*

Suicide is rare? I thought it was common in women who were refused abortion.

This is an oft-repeated fallacy. Suicide among pregnant women is extremely rare. Several well-controlled studies have shown this conclusively.

The State of Ohio had only 2 maternal suicide deaths between the years 1955-1963.

Ohio State Med. Journal, Dec. 1966, P. 1294, MATERNAL DEATHS INVOLVING SUICIDE.

Between 1938 and 1958, over 13,500 Swedish women were refused abortions. Only three committed suicide.

J. Ottosson, LEGAL ABORTION IN SWEDEN, J. Biosocial Sciences, 3, 173, 1971

In Brisbane, Australia, no pregnant woman has ever committed suicide.

F. Whitlock & J. Edwards, PREGNANCY & ATTEMPTED SUICIDE, Comp. Psychiatry, 1968, 9, 1

In Birmingham, England, in seven years, 119 women under fifty, committed suicide, none were pregnant.

M. Sim, ABORTION & THE PSYCHIATRIST Br. Med. J. 1963, 2, 145

Give more details

In a detailed report of the Minnesota experience from 1950-65 entitled *"Criminal Abortion Deaths, Il-*

legitimate Pregnancy Deaths, and Suicides in Pregnancy†" the following facts are reported:

— There were only 14 maternal suicides in the state of Minnesota in 15 years, or one for every 93,000 live births. Four were first pregnancies. None were illegitimately pregnant.

— Ten of these women committed suicide after delivery, only four while pregnant, leading to the author's comment, *"The fetus in utero must be a protective mechanism. Perhaps women are reluctant to take another life with them when they do this."*

— Twelve of the 14 were psychotic depressions. Two were schitzophrenics. Only four had seen a psychiatrist.

— Male suicides during these years averaged 16 per 100,000 population. Non-pregnant female suicides averaged 3.5 per 100,000 and pregnant female suicides 0.6 per 100,00.

— The authors conclude that therapeutic abortion for psychiatric reasons *"seems a most nebulous, non-objective non-scientific approach to medicine. It would seem that psychiatrists would accomplish more by using the available modalities of their speciality in the treatment or rehabilitation of the patient instead of recommending the destruction of another one."*

Minnesota Maternal Mortality Committee,
Dept. of OB & Gyn, University of Minnesota.
†American Journal of OB & Gyn, 6/1/67

But shouldn't psychiatrists know best?

What usually happens is that the psychiatrist, who should be capable of helping the woman through her pregnancy by virtue of his skill, may advise an abortion. This doesn't cure the psychiatric illness, being at best only symptomatic treatment. Most commonly, after such an encounter, there is no follow-up psychiatric treatment. To most inquiring minds, this would seem to confirm the fact that there was no major mental illness in the first place.

Are you saying that "mental illness" is usually just an excuse for an abortion?

We are saying exactly that.

But don't several physicians usually have to certify that there is mental ilness?

In practice, the need for certification by several physicians (psychiatrists or non-psychiatrists) to authorize an abortion has been a blatant, premeditated, open-door vehicle by which abortion-on-demand has come to be a reality. Any physician can find three other physcans who will sign a document testifying to the need for an abortion for mental health. Any physician can also find three other physicians who would never sign such a document. This requirement has proved to be totally meaningless.

What if a woman has a psychosis, is pregnant, and needs shock treatment. Shouldn't she be aborted?

Pregnancy does not rule out the use of almost any known psychiatric therapy, including electric shock.

But don't some women have psychotic breakdowns after delivering a baby?

Yes. Postpartum psychosis is relatively common following childbirth. It, however, is almost entirely unpredictable. It does not bear any particular relationship to whether or not a woman had mental trouble during her pregnancy. It frequently occurs in a woman who was entirely mentally stable during her pregnancy. Furthermore these "after the baby blues" are rarely permanent and seldom have relapses.

Are there post-abortion psychoses?

Yes and compared to post-delivery disturbances they are much more serious, last longer and are more likely to recur. They are more often the "hard" cases.

Sim, M. 1963. Abortion and the Psychiatrist, Brit. Med. J. 2: 145-148.

What of post-abortion suicide?

In 35 months, Suiciders Anonymous in Cincinnati counseled 5620 who had attempted suicide. Of the 4000 who were female, over 1800 had had abortions.

Meta Uchtman, Testimony Sept. 1, 1981, Cincinnati City Council.

A British study reporting on eight maternal abortion deaths, noted that two of them were suicide deaths, after the abortion.

British Medical, Journal, May, 1970

Do these guilt feelings come from religious beliefs?

Certainly there are guilt feelings relating to religious beliefs, but most guilt feelings subsequent to abortion have little to do with sectarian religious belief. Abortion violates something very basic in a woman's nature. She normally is the giver of life. Most women who are pregnant are quite aware of the fact that they have a baby growing within them. Most women who have an abortion feel that they have killed their baby. Sometimes there is an almost irresolvable guilt, continuing self reproach, and depression. A good counselor would be of help to a woman during a trying time like this, but the woman who has had an abortion doesn't always come to a counselor.

A wise psychiatrist has said that it is easier to scrape the baby out of the mother's womb than to scrape the thought of that baby out of her mind.

Are there any good studies reporting on mental health damage from abortion?

"The incidence of serious permanent psychiatric

aftermath [from abortion] is variously reported as being from between 9 and 59%."

Council, Royal College of OB & Gyn, England, 1966

How about in the United States?

Dr. Paul Gebhart, who did the pioneering work in human sexuality with Dr. Alfred Kinsey and who is known as one of the foremost authorities in this field in the United States, in testifying before the New Jersey legislature in 1968, said that there was evidence of prolonged psychiatric trauma in 9% of a sample of American women who had abortion induced therapeutically or criminally.

I'm not sure that much of this guilt business isn't an unconscious replay of old Christian ethics. How about a non-Christian culture?

Japan has had abortion-on-demand for 22 years and is certainly not a Christian culture. Three major studies in the past decade have asked about guilt.

In 1963, the Aichi survey reported that 73.1% of women who had been aborted felt "anguish" about what they did.

In 1964, Dr. Tatsuo Kaseki's report stated that 59% felt that abortion was something "very evil" and only 8% thought that it was not "something bad".

In 1969, a major survey by the Prime Minister's Office reported that 88% of women answered that abortion is "bad."

Can you predict who will have psychiatric problems resulting from abortion?

A good evaluation of this comes from Dr. M. Ekblad in Sweden, which as we know, is a country with very liberal sexual morality standards. Abortion there is not subject to any moral stigma. Dr. Ekblad, however, found that 25% of women having legal abortions later had "serious regret". In evaluating who might have emotional problems because of abortion, he found a clear relationship. *"The psychiatrically abnormal woman finds it more difficult than the psychologically normal woman to stand the stress of abortion."*

M. Ekblad, ACTA SCANDINAVICA, 1955

The World Health Organization, in an offical statement in 1970, said: *"Serious mental disorders arise more often in women with previous mental problems. Thus the very women for whom legal abortion is considered justified on psychiatric grounds are the ones who have the highest risk of post-abortion psychiatric disorders."*

Meyerowitz et al also conclude that psychologically disturbed women do less well emotionally after abortion.

INDUCED ABORTION FOR PSYCHIATRIC REASONS,
American Journal of Psychiatry, 127:9, 1971

So did Dr. Chas. Ford and associates at U.C.L.A. *". . . The more serious the psychiatric diagnosis, the less beneficial was the abortion."*

ABORTION, IS IT A THERAPEUTIC PROCEDURE IN PSYCHIATRY?,
Ford et al, Journal Am. Med. Assn., November 22, 1971.

A survey carried out in Birmingham showed that emotionally disturbed girls under the age of sixteen who were aborted suffered greater psychiatric distrubances than emotionally disturbed girls of the same age who were refused abortions. The very fact of motherhood appeared to have stabilizing effect on the girls who continued through pregnancy.

Myre Sims, M.D., F.R.C. Psych.
Prof. Psychological Medicine
United Birmingham Hospitals, England

Then the woman in poor mental health is more likely to suffer further psychological harm than the woman who is not upset?

This truism has been a rather well-kept secret.

Emotional upset, anxiety, fear, strain, and mixed feelings about pregnancy are common, even under the best of circumstances. Pregnancy is not a minor event. Feelings of depression in the early stages of pregnancy are very common. Judgments that the pregnancy and child are unwanted are very common. What is absolutely crucial to understand, however, is that how a woman feels early in her pregnancy and how she will feel after delivery are often completely different. If all upset women with unwanted pregnancies had been aborted in years past, at least one-third of our readers would not be living today.

Competent medical opinion is deeply divided as to whether psychiatric reasons ever justify an abortion. The phrase "mental health," written into some of our laws, has opened a Pandora's box of abortion-on-demand.

How long after an abortion can Psychological Problems occur?

There is no time limit. An example can tell often more than many scientific papers. Your author will never forget — A 44 year old lady who had been childless during her marriage. A Christian woman with a Jewish husband, they had been unable to adopt a child because of their mixed religion. She longed for a child but was sterile as several tests had shown her tubes to be blocked. Theirs was an excellent marriage and both had given of themselves to many community and charitable efforts. On this day, after a routine exam, I told her that, because of a continuing fibroid enlargement, her uterus would have to be removed.

She gasped as if hit by a pole, and collapsed in a hysterical heap, completely out of control in her grief and crying.

After considerable time, sedatives and support, I was able to again talk with her and the story tumbled out. She related how she had become pregnant while in college and had had an abortion "by an excellent surgeon." She had been sterilized by the abortion. Throughout her subsequent marriage, she had hoped against hope that somehow she would still concieve. Now I had just told her that her womb must be removed and her last, faint hope for a baby was forever gone.

Through tear reddened eyes and with a pathos that still brings a lump into my throat, she quietly said, *"I killed the only baby I ever bore."*

8

UNWANTED PREGNANCIES

> *"Editor:*
>
> *I would like to write to you to let you know that I am in full accord with the abortions that are being performed in New York City. For every early physiologic process interrupted, we are preventing a candidate for our relief rolls, our prison population, and our growing list of unwanted and frequently battered children."*

The above, taken from a letter to the editor of the A.M.A. News, reflects the thinking of some people today. If the above were true, the proponents of abortion at the mother's request would certainly have added weight to their side of the balance arm of the scale weighing the value of the life of the unborn child. If the above is not true, then pro-abortionists have deluded themselves with more wishful thinking.

I believe every child should be a wanted child, don't you?

We agree that every child should be wanted. A world with only wanted children would be an idyllic place in which to live. No one could quarrel with that as an idealistic goal. Wouldn't it also be a wonderful world if there were no unwanted wives by husbands, no aging parents unwanted by their children, no unwanted Jews, black people, Catholics, Chicanos, or ever again a person who at one time or place finds himself unwanted or persecuted. Let's all try to achieve this, but also remember that people have clay feet and, sadly, the unwanted will probably always be with us.

To use being wanted by someone as a measure of whether a human life is allowed to live is a frightening concept as, sadly, its converse logically awaits us — that the unwanted can be eliminated. Don't forget, Hitler's Germany was ideal for wanted Aryans

"Every Child a Wanted Child" should be completed with "and if not wanted, kill!" for that is exactly what that Planned Parenthood slogan means.

But why should a mother carry to term an unwanted pregnancy?

Physicians who deliver babies will all agree that a significant percentage of all pregnancies are not planned, and, at the time these women are first seen in the doctor's office, they definitely have "unwanted pregnancies." Overwhelmingly, however, a mother adjusts to the initial surprise and shock, accepts the baby growing within her, and comes to anticipate the birth of her child. After more than twenty years of medical practice, your author personally can say without hesitancy that he has seen many unwanted pregnancies, but has yet to see the first unwanted newborn child. If we permit abortion for an unwanted pregnancy, we will be destroying vast numbers of children, who, by the time of their birth and through their childhood would have been very dearly wanted and deeply loved children indeed. If the judgment of being wanted at an early stage of pregnancy were a final judgment, and abortions were permitted freely, a high percentage of everyone reading this book would never have been born.

But what if a mother delivered a baby that she really didn't want?

The federal judges who ruled the Ohio abortion law to be constitutional spoke very eloquently to this.

> *"Equating the necessity of giving birth to a child with the necessity of rearing the child has no foundation in law or fact. The law may take permanently from its natural parents a child who is neglected by them, and the frequent hesitancy of courts and social agencies in this regard does not change the legal situation. Statutes of practically all states provide for the voluntary surrender of children. When the statutes are complied with, the child is legally and practically as dead to its natural parents as if it had been aborted, stillborn, or had died in infancy. The validity and effectiveness of surrender statutes has been upheld in every case in which they have been questioned. There is no need for parents to terminate an undesired pregnancy by killing the unborn child physically when with less risk to themselves, its legal death can so easily be procured."*

U.S. Dist. Court, Northern District of Ohio,
Steinberg vs Rhodes, C70-289, Jan. 1971.

The opening letter assumes that all unwanted pregnancies will be neglected children. Is that a valid assumption?

That assumption is almost too naive and simplistic to be given any serious consideration. The fact that it has been mentioned again and again is almost beyond comprehension. Most unwanted pregnancies become wanted babies. Some wanted pregnancies become unwanted ones. Unloved babies sometimes become dearly loved and vice versa. To make the assumption that, because a woman is unwillingly pregnant, the child in every case, in most cases, or even in many cases will be unwanted and therefore neglected and abused, is totally inaccurate and wildly unrealistic. Some will, of course, but many will not. Why kill them all before birth? Why not sort them out after birth, strengthen the laws of our courts as mentioned above, and take unwanted children from parents who are unworthy to raise them?

Can you substantiate this?

A number of important studies have been done on women with a) very wanted, and b) very unwanted pregnancies. Their attitudes during pregnancy were compared with their love of their baby after birth.

> *"It is clear that mothers who initially believed their pregnancy to be 'the worst thing that ever happened to them' came to feel about the same degree of affection for their children as the mothers who were initially 'ecstatic' about the pregnancy."*

> *"Most women who were most regretful of the pregnancy now claim they would have the child again if given the opportunity." Whereas ". . . one of every six mothers who were initially pleased with pregnancy would choose not to have the child again."*

> *They conclude "Initial feelings about pregnancy are predictive of how a mother will eventually feel about her child to only a very limited degree."*

> How Much do Mothers Love Their Children,
> P. Cameron et al, Rocky-Mt. Psychological Assn.,
> May 12, 1972.

> *"There is a contention that unwanted conceptions tend to have undesirable effects . . . the direct evidence for such a relationship is almost completely lacking, except for a few fragments of retrospective evidence. It was the hope of this article to find more convincing*

systematic research evidence and to give some idea of the amount of relationship between unwanted conception and undesired effect on children. This hope has been disappointed."

E. Pohlman, UNWANTED CONCEPTION,
RESEARCH ON UNDESIRABLE CONSEQUENCES.
Eugenics Quarterly 14, (1967) 143

Dr. Ferriera found no relationship between unplanned pregnancies and newborn deviant behavior. In fact, there were more deviant babies of mothers who had planned their pregnancy than those who had not.

A.J. Ferriera, THE PREGNANT WOMAN'S EMOTIONAL ATTITUDE AND ITS
REFLECTION IN THE NEWBORN
Am. J. Orthopsychiat, 30 (1960), 553

Others have conclusively demonstrated a spontaneous change from pre-partum rejection to postpartum acceptance of their children by a group of mothers.

M. Zemlich, R. Watson, MATERNAL
ATTITUDES OF ACCEPTANCE AND REJECTION
DURING AND AFTER PREGNANCY.
Am. J. Orthopsychiat, 23 (1953) 570

Don't some studies prove the opposite?

No! In the entire world literature on this subject there are only two studies that attempt to show that there is a negative effect on the children who had been "unwanted pregnancies."

The first study from Sweden was shown by Professor Paul Cameron to be invalid and the second one, published in Family Planning Perspectives was scathingly discredited by Dr. Samuel Nigro. Both studies had the same fault, that of selecting a study group that had such a percent of unstable mothers that the problems in the children could have been predicted whether or not the unwantedness had entered the picture or not.

What of other countries?

— Japan has had abortion on demand for over twenty years. It is used there as a method of birth control, but "cases of infanticide have been increasing so much that social workers have made appeals to Japanese mothers in newspapers and on television not to kill their babies."

The Sunday Times
June 23, 1974

— When Rumania reversed its law on abortion in 1966, doctors stated that not only had they *not* overcome the problem of unwanted children — but that one of the factors which had caused some of them to urge for changes in the law was that there had been such an increase in the number of psychiatric cases amongst lonely only children and children of neurotic mothers.

— In England the Working Party of the Royal College of Obstetricians and Gynecologists stated that the vast majority of unplanned pregnancies become wanted children.

— Aberdeen, Scotland is a unique city because, through an unusual law it has had open abortion for 20 years in a nation that has had legal abortion only one third as long. If the availability of abortion did reduce unwanted children, it should have the best record in Britain. In fact, it has the worse record, with 10.2/1000 abandoned, abused and uncared for children being cared for by public agencies compared with the national average of 6.6.

Annual Report, Chief Medical Health Officer
Aberdeen, Scotland, 1972

— Child abuse in the U.S. has risen in direct proportion to the increase in numbers of abortions. For example, Colorado's Vital Statistics show

	abortions	child abuse
1969	946	114
1974	8.964	866

Denver Post, 9-14-75

But don't many unwanted pregnancies become battered children?

Many would think so. In fact, this is not true. Dr. Edward Lenoski is continuing a study of over 600 battered children who have come to his medical center. He has found that 91% of the battered children in his study were planned pregnancies. Ninety one percent is far above average for planned pregnancies. Most of our readers undoubtedly deeply cherish and love the children that they have been given. How many, however, actually planned the conception of 91% of them? We could apparently kill all "unwanted" babies in the early stages of pregnancy, but still not significantly reduce the numbers of battered children.

> Edward Lenoski, Prof. Pediatrics
> University of Southern California

He has also found that, since the advent of the contraceptive pill, (which has certainly reduced unwanted pregnancies), child beating is up threefold.

— Parents who abuse children showed the wantedness of the child in several ways. The women wore maternity clothes earlier and 24% named the children after themselves (as compared to 4% of a control group), while 90.3% of the children were legitimate.

> E. Lenoski, Nat'l Right to Life News, Jan. '75

— The parents commonly

> *"Grew up in a hostile environment, and were abused themselves." .... "When the children fail to satisfy their [unrealistic, neurotic expectations of perfection] emotional needs, the parent react with the same violence they experienced as children."*

> Jas. Walsh, Ill. Dept. of Child and Fam. Services
> Newsweek, July 24, 1972

What of the right of a woman to the privacy of her own body?

The U.S. Supreme Court decision is based on this. We think it is an entirely fallacious bit of reasoning. If you, as a citizen, stand outside of a door and listen to a mother battering her child, even to the point of killing him, what would you do? Would you respect the privacy of her home? You would not! You would open or break down the door and rescue the child. By virtue of her assault upon and abuse of another human person, she has surrendered her constitutional right to privacy in this case. The same analogy applies to abortion. The right of the child to live is greater than and supersedes any right that a woman may have to the privacy of her own body.

But a woman does have a right to her own body. Isn't the child, at least in the early stages of pregnancy, part of her body?

A woman's appendix, obviously a part of her body, can be removed for sufficient reason. The cells of the appendix, however, carry the identical genetic code that is present in every other cell in the mother's body. They are, for this reason, undeniably part of her body. The single-celled fertilized ovum or later developing embryonic human being within her uterus cannot, by any stretch of the imagination, be considered part of her body. This new living being has a genetic code that is totally different from the cells of the mother's body. He or she is, in truth, a completely separate growing human being and can never be considered part of the mother's body. Does she have a right to her own body? Yes. But this is not part of her own body. It is another person's body.

No right at all?

The Rev. Charles Carroll, Protestant chaplain of the University of California at Berkeley, student of International Law at Yale, Harvard and the University of Berlin during the Hitler period, and officer of the United States military government in Germany at the trial of the Nazi doctors at Nuremberg, has stated:

> "As I would reject the law of pater-familias of ancient Rome, so I would also re-

ject the proposed law of materfamilias in present day America. As I would not sympathize with the grant by the state of the power of life and death of his offspring to the Roman father, so I cannot sympathize with the grant by any state of the power of life and death over her offspring to the American mother. Surely I would hope our legislators would be as humane as the Emperor Hadrian, who abolished that article of the Roman Law."

———   ———   ———   ———   ———

We believe that:

A nation and its people will ultimately be judged, not by the fact that there are unwanted ones amongst them, but by what is done for them.

are they cared for?
or
are they killed?

"Amen, I say to you 'what you have done to these, the least of my brethern, you have done to me.'"

9

POPULATION EXPLOSION?

— *Births below replacement rate since 1973*

— *"If you're a businessman, this chart may be the shape of your future. It shows how the birthrate in the U.S. has been declining until now it's below the rate of replacement. This will have tremendous economic, social and political repercussions." (See Fig. XI)*

Where Have All The Babies Gone?
Forbes Magazine, Sept. 1972

One of the major reasons given to justify new permissive abortion laws is the pressure of unwanted population. Let's look at some of these facts.

What is the population of the United States?

The 1980 U.S. Census count placed the U.S. population at 226 million.

Wasn't this a substantial increase in the last decade?

Yes, but fewer people were added to our population in the decade of the 60's than in the decade of the 50's. In the percentage of gain, it was the second lowest rate of increase of any decade in the history of the United States. The rate through the 1970's was the lowest yet.

How many children should the average family have in order to stabilize population growth?

In 1850 the average number of children per family in the U.S. was 6.0. In 1957, it was 3.76. In 1970, it was 2.45. By 1973, it had dropped to 1.8 and has remained there. Replacement level is 2.11. The previous all time low had been during the great depression. It bottomed in 1930 at 2.25.

The birthrate, the number of babies born per 1000 population has dropped to between 15.0 and 16.0. Even in the depth of the 1930-40 depression, it only went down to 18.0.

But might the growth rate go back up again?

"The long-term direction of the U.S. birthrate is still downward. Overall fertility in the U.S. as well as the rest of the world is at an all time low."

P. Glick, U.S. Census Bureau, May 1, 1978,
Dept. HEW

The prestigious financial monthly, Forbes, has said *"There are those who think the birthrate will rise again, but the trend of history is against them. Ironing out temporary squiggles like that after World War II, the U.S. birthrate has trended down since around 1800."*

Where Have All The Babies Gone?
Forbes Magazine, p. 37, Sept. 1972

How many babies are actually born in the United States in a year?

In 1957, there were 4,308,000 babies born. In 1979, there were 3,330,000 babies born. We are already educating that excess of births from the late Fifties. Our schools are crowded with them. This

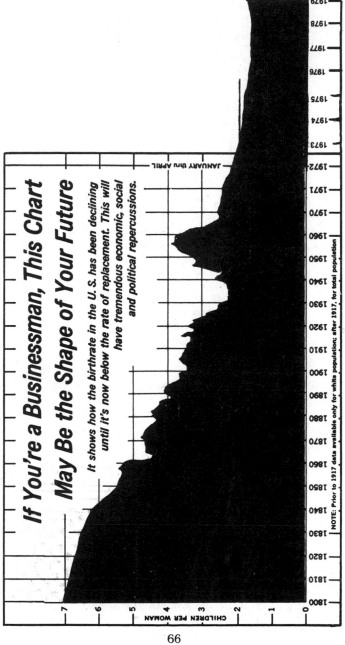

If You're a Businessman, This Chart May Be the Shape of Your Future

It shows how the birthrate in the U. S. has been declining until it's now below the rate of replacement. This will have tremendous economic, social and political repercussions.

JANUARY thru APRIL

CHILDREN PER WOMAN

7 6 5 4 3 2 1 0

1800 1810 1820 1830 1840 1850 1860 1870 1880 1890 1900 1910 1920 1930 1940 1950 1960 1970 1971 1972 1973 1974 1975 1976 1977 1978 1979

NOTE: Prior to 1917 data available only for white population; after 1917, for total population

Fig. XI With permission Forbes Magazine Sept 1, 1972.

66

bulge is passing, however. In 1980, for instance, there were 1,500,000 fewer third graders in the nation's classrooms than there had been. We have an overabundance of teachers, schools, and educational facilities in our nation.

You believe that families will be smaller in the future?

In a Gallup Poll the question was asked: *"Would you like four or more children in your family?"*

> *in 1967 — 40% answered "Yes"*
> *in 1971 — 23% answered "Yes"*
> *in 1974 — 19% answered "Yes"*

Of great importance was that, of all the college-educated, only 14% wanted four or more. Of those with only a grade school education, 33% wanted four or more.

This is further confirmation, if any is needed, that the only way to effectively limit population growth is to raise a group's standard of living and education.

Limit Population By Raising The Standard of Living?

Yes, even John D. Rockefeller III has said "After forty years of advocacy of family planning as a primary approach to world population, I have now changed my mind. The evidence has been mounting, particularly in the past decade, to indicate that family planning is not enough.

This new approach recognizes that rapid population growth is only one among many problems facing most countries; that it is a multiplier and intensifier of other problems rather than a cause of them. It recognizes that motivation for family planning is best stimulated by hope that living conditions and opportunities in general will improve."

U.N. Conf. on Population, Bucharest 1976

If the birth rate is dropping, why does the total population continue to grow?

Immigation accounts for perhaps 50% of the growth. Also, the number of old people in the dying age-group is still only two-thirds of the number of people being born. The present continuing population growth will cease in a few years when the population bulge reaches old age. At present rates there will then be more people dying than being born and the population will decline.

What of the death rate? Does this influence population size?

The U.S. death rate is now 8.9 per 1,000 people per year. As our population grows older and more people reach old age, the death rate will eventually double to almost 20 per 1,000 per year, assuming our life expectancy holds at 70 years. In forty years there will be twice as many Americans 65 years or older than there are today, but far fewer younger taxpayers.

Remember, in determining population growth or decline one should not compare babies born to grandparents dying. Rather one must compare replacement of the current number of reproductive age individuals with the number of babies being born, as only this measures the ultimate growth or decline of a population. By this accurate measurement, the Western world is now in a sharp population decline.

A major population think tank has predicted "An America in 2000 A.D. where half the population is over 50 yrs., and a third over 65."

F. Domville, THE POPULATION CRASH,
Population Crisis Council, Chicago.

Translate this into U.S. workers compared to retirees

In 1980, 100 workers supported 30 retirees. In the year 2000 it will still be 33. By 2020 however, 100 workers will have to support 47 retired persons through social security and by 2040, 100 workers will have to support 64 retirees—that is if birth rates stay where they are.

Biblical Economics Today, Nov. 1978

How long will fewer and fewer younger workers be willing to pay higher and higher taxes for a higher and higher percent of retired oldsters? Or could it be, that having been taught that killing off the burdensome ones is an answer, that euthanasia will become their answer?

What about population trends? Can't they tell us accurately what will happen?

Population trends are notoriously subject to both mistakes and abuse in predicting any distance in the future.

— In 1910, there were 30.1 children born in the United States for every 1000 people. In 1936, this had dropped to 18.4. If this trend had continued, births in the United States would have ceased altogether by 1975.

— In 1936, the birth rate was 18.4 per 1000. In 1957, the birth rate had risen to 25.3 per 1000. If this trend had continued, we would have had over 400 million people by the year 2000, almost a billion by 2050, and two-and-a-half billion by 2100.

— In 1957, the birth rate was 25.3 per 1000. By 1974, it had dropped to 14.9. If this trend continues, the last baby in the United States to ever utter its first cry after birth, will be born in the year 1990, and further births will cease totally.

It seems obvious that extending any population trend very far into the future can prove to be quite inaccurate.

How much space is there actually existing at this time for every person who lives in the United States?

If we divide the number of people presently living in the United States by its total acreage, each individual has ten acres.

What percentage of the population of the U.S. is needed to produce the food we eat?

Less than 2%, but we feed 25% of the people on the earth.

What of the world population? Will it follow the same trends as the United States?

One thing is certain. Neither voluntary birth control nor abortion has ever stopped the population growth of an economically undeveloped and underprivileged country. One sure way to slow down population growth of underdeveloped countries is to bring them up to an increased standard of living. As we increase the standard of living of a nation, its people will voluntarily limit their family size. This is the major problem for the rest of the world in the decades ahead.

> *"Limited evidence shows that there is a proportionately larger falling birthrate in areas touched by the Green Revolution, compared to those untouched by it."*

> *"If indeed higher agricultural productivity does directly encourage lower fertility, then FAO's main contribution to population policy may well be to push its efforts in agricultural development at an even more rapid pace than at present."*

> Food and Agricultural Organization, United Nations
> A. H. Boerma, Director General

> THE GREEN REVOLUTION, P. Scott,
> Twin Circle, April 23, 1972.

If the current sharp decline (since 1955) in the world birth rate continues (and they think it will) the U. S. Agency for International Development states that *"It should be possible to reduce the world crude birth rate to less than 20 and the world population growth rate to less than 1% per year by 1980,"* i.e. to the general levels of present day Europe and the U.S.

World Fertility Trends During the 1960's
Ravenholt, Brackett, & Chao, Toronto, April 1972

"After all the rhetoric called forth by the fact that the U.N. declared 1974 a 'World Population Year,' a look at the actual global statistics comes as something of a shock. According to a study by the U.S. Agency for International Development, in 72 of the 82 countries with reliable statistics, rich and poor, African, Asian, and European, birth rates are declining."

Wall Street Journal, Dec. 16, 1974

Abortion is being spoken of as a means of population control. What does the medical profession think of this?

The official statement of the American College of Obstetrics and Gynecology in 1968 said: *"It is firmly stated that the College will not condone nor support the concept that abortion be considered or performed as a means of population control."*

What of overpopulation and crowding and its deleterious influence on human behavior?

In Holland, the population density is 1,000 people per square mile. In the United States it is 57 people per square mile. Even taking into account the vast waste areas of mountains, etc. in the United States, the only areas that approach Holland in population density are those of our crowded cities. Yet it is well known that Holland has only a fraction of the crime rate and social upset of our major cities, and was the nation where most Europeans would prefer to live, according to a recent poll.

As another example, Great Britain has 50 million people living in an area smaller than California. Why is it then, that there are fewer murders on the entire British Isles annually than there are in the city of Chicago, or Cleveland, or even of Greater Kansas City? Obviously, population density in itself does not produce high crime rates and social upset.

Even Dr. Paul Erlich has said: *"There is little re-lationship between the density of an area and the amount of crime or mental illness. When the eco-nomic levels of the areas are equated, density has no effect on juvenile delinquency."*

JOURNAL OF APPLIED PSYCHOLOGY, Vol. I, 1971

Won't too many people increase the problem of pollution?

Certainly, more people produce more pollution. Certainly, more affluent people produce more pollu-tion per person than poor people. However, more wealthy and more educated people also produce the wealth and technology to combat pollution. The ba-sic problem is not the simple fact of people existing, but of education, of methods of industrial production, of self-discipline, etc. Most pollution problems made their appearance or became very much worse in the years following World War II. Since 1946, the U.S. population has risen by 42%, pollution by as much as 2,000% (non-returnable pop bottles by 53,000%). Thus, to advocate abortion as a solution to the U.S.'s en-vironmental problem *"is equivalent to attempting to save a leaking ship by lightening the load and forcing passengers overboard. One is constrained to ask if there isn't something radically wrong with the ship."*

THE CLOSING CIRCLE, B. Commoner, Knopf, 1971

What will remedy our pollution problems?

Not merely the simplistic answer of reducing the number of children per family. We could stop popu-lation growth, and our rivers would still be ecological slums, the air over our cities would still remain un-breathable, and our environment would continue to deteriorate. What is needed is massive efforts, great sums of money, educational campaigns, and in many ways, a substantial change in the way we live, not in how many of us are alive.

How much of the U.S. pollution problem is due to the automobile and how much to people?

The number of automobiles is growing twice as

fast as people. They contribute 75% of our urban air pollution, and are a major factor in depletion of our natural resources. Highways consume 200,000 acres of land annually, displacing 56,000 people annually from their homes. In 1969 America had a net gain of 2,084,000 people, but 3,835,000 cars. *"We can no longer tolerate the reckless and haphazard proliferation of automobiles. Our cities are suffering from an increasingly acute 'autosclerosis'. Eventually, hopefully sooner rather than later, we must achieve zero automobile growth."*

Autos and People — Room for Both?,
T. Germann, America, April 15, 1972.

What about the two billion people in the world who go to bed hungry every night?

This is a completely inaccurate figure. It speaks to the level of malnutrition, not to a level of hunger. Malnutrition is often cultural, being based on poor eating habits, and is in no way starvation. Roger Revelle, a Harvard population expert, has given us firm figures that illustrate that deaths from undernutrition throughout the world have been declining for several decades in the face of rising population.

Family Planning Perspectives, April, 1971, p. 67

Won't the rest of the world outgrow its food supply?

— Within the last several years, a "green revolution" has occurred. Hybrid wheat, corn, and rice have been developed that have radically changed the outlook in these hungry lands. In Pakistan, wheat output had soared from four-and-a-half to twelve-and-a-half million tons in just five years. In India, wheat production has gone from twelve-and-a-half to nineteen-and-a-half million tons in five years. The same has happened to rice within several years. At present rates, most of the sub-continent of Asia will be exporting grain rather than needing our help to stave off starvation. [India in 1972 had a grain surplus of eight million tons.] Their remaining problem is distribution of food, not production of it.

It is estimated that the world's farmers can theoretically feed a population 40 times as large as todays.

Prof. Donald Bogue, Time Magazine, Sept. 13, 1971

— In 1860 beef production in Southern U.S. averaged six pounds of live weight grain per acre per year. In 1900 with carpet grass it was 30 lbs. In 1930 a new grass doubled this to 60 lbs. In 1940 with nitrogen fertilizer it reached 150 lbs. and by 1945 was 275 lbs. By 1948 more fertilizer raised it to 675 lbs., and in 1970 a new grass and less fertilizer shot it up to 1000 lbs. per acre. Today with the Coast Cross I strain plus fertilizer the yield is 3000 lbs. Tomorrow?

The Miracle of Grass, G. Carter,
Twin Circle, April 9, 1972.

— *"Ironically but fortunately, it is the nations with the most rapidly growing recent food deficits which also possess the greatest capacity for increased production. . . For example, worldwide, 42% of potentially arable land is cropped, but in Latin America only 17% is used."* He also noted that while increasing food production in the past always meant to increase the land area farmed, today increasingly *"the crop yield can be increased."*

Henry Kissinger, AP report 1974
World Food conference, Rome

Let's take Latin American slums, don't they have too many people?

"Latin America is visibly under-populated. Great tracts of good land are lying uninhabited, or only very sparsely cultivated. The economics of most of the Latin American countries are suffering acutely from shortages of skilled labor, which they have accentuated by following xenophobic nationalistic policies of restricting immigration, even from neighbouring countries."

"Latin America's troubles — which are serious — are due to mis-government. Nearly all the Latin

*American republics have permitted the excessive
growth of their capital cities, with all the attendant
problems of slums, water supply, hygiene, crime, etc.,
when they should have been pursuing active policies
of decentralization. Many of them are dominated by
land-owning aristocracies, who make no serious effort
to develop their properties, and who evade their due
share of taxation . . . Their industries are at very low
levels of productivity, and enjoy excessive tariff protection. What a marvelous let-out it is for the incompetent and corrupt politicians who administer these
countries to say that their troubles are all due to population growth. Check population growth in order to
give us breathing space to deal with our problems,
they plead. A breathing space is the last thing that
they should have. It will only lead to further postponement of problems which should have been tack-
led years ago. These politicians should be made to
face their responsibilities."*

POPULATION GROWTH — THE ADVANTAGES.
Colin Clark

But what of predictions of imminent catastrophy such as from the Club of Rome?

"Garbage in, garbage out" sums it up in the com-
puter programers words. Colin Clark in his book
POPULATION GROWTH totally debunks their alarmist
predictions by showing some amazing errors in the
material fed into their computers.

But what of 1974's famines in Southwest Asia and the Sahara area?

No one knows these answers. The Sahara drought
was an act of God which no one could control. A
good bit of the problem is due to over grazing of too
many animals and lack of any government policies of
soil conservation, etc.

India would be exporting grain except for the political and economic policies of the oil producing

countries, making fertilizer and petroleum too expensive.

Bengladesh is one of the richest agricultural lands in the world but has an unbelieveable degree of lack of development and economic and social chaos. Partly due to war, to floods and typhoons, to politics, etc., there is no solution in sight.

The point to be made is there are all kinds of major problems and often population is only a minor problem if at all.

Shouldn't people be encouraged, then, to have less children?

"Most poor people in the Third World don't have unemployment pay, sickness benefits, or old-age pensions. And when jobs are scarce, illness common, and old age comes early, children are necessary for protection, security and peace of mind. As Milkah Singh, an Indian farmer told one researcher: 'Without our children God knows what would happen to me and their mother when we are too old to work and earn.'"

New Internationalist
May, 1974

What is the answer then to the huge problem of poverty if it is not related to population growth?

Aaron Segal in his book "The Rich, the Poor and Population" says that *"the road back to population sanity involves a few, simple, unpleasant truths."*

1) People are not poor because they have too many children.
2) A decision to reduce the birth rate of a given society can only be taken by the members of that society in response to their needs. Children play only a marginal role.
3) Trade, aid, immigration, income distribution, education, and maternal health,

have much more to do with reducing the birth rate than coercive birth control.

4) The rich world could really help by paying fairer prices for raw materials and buying more cheap labor-intensive manufactured goods from the poor world.

5) It would be helpful also if the population foundations (such as International Planned Parenthood) would do something for the true needs of these people instead of offering them only the simplistic one of population control.

6) At present, family planning agencies are little more than the rich man's lackey — trying to prove in true Victorian style that the poor are responsible for their own conditions. The rich should concern themselves with the real causes of poverty in their own countries as well as in the Third World, rather than relying on population control as a form of conservation social control.

7) If we cannot help to create proper conditions in which individuals will want to reduce the size of their families, then we have absolutely no moral right to coerce by any means whatsoever.

Finally — Remember always a balance is needed. Don't be too critical of developed nations.

— The U.S.A. with 6% of the world's people consumes 30% of the world's resources — but it also produces 48% of the world's output.

— The U.S.A. with one-tenth of 1% of the world's population employed on its farms feeds 25% of the world's people.

— Consider Russia with 50%, China with 80% of its people needed to produce food, think of the potential if nations can be developed?

10

MOTHERS
DIE FROM
ABORTIONS?

— No one will ever know how many —
At least not from American and Canadian reports

Why not!

Abortion deaths and complications are simply not reported as such. They are listed as other problems. If an abortionist perforates a womb and the mother gets a pelvic abscess and dies, the cause may be listed as "D & C, perforation, sepsis and death." Her hemorrhage and blood transfusions following a suction abortion elsewhere is listed by her own local physician as "abnormal bleeding, D & C."

Why is this?

Typically a woman goes to a large city or to a profit making abortion chamber for an abortion. She returns home to bleed, become infected, etc. Usually, she is saved but sometimes she dies. The family will then plead with her doctor, "Please don't mark abortion on the chart. People will find out and her (our) reputation will be ruined." Most compassionate physicians, will not want to hurt her any further and will not quite tell all on the records.

Give an example.

Recently, when your authors were speaking at a Midwestern city, a college doctor in the audience stated that she hadn't seen any abortion complications. With great ire a greying man arose, identified himself as a busy local gynecologist and said *"Margaret, that's a lie and you know it. I have been referring your students for abortion but I'm here tonight to state that I'll never refer another. The complications I've been seeing have made me sick, and then a poor girl last week — I cannot tell her story as I mean to protect her — but it was a disaster!"*

We asked the doctor if he had been reporting these abortion complications and he replied *"report? never! Someone might find out. These poor girls have suffered enough."*

You mean that even maternal deaths are not reported accurately?

Yes! Illegal ones usually are reported. No, legal ones are seldom reported. Here's the story.

The woman who has an illegal abortion and then bleeds or gets infected will not go back to the illegal abortionist for care. She will go to a community or university hospital for care and be seen by a new physician. If she dies, this new physician has no reason to falsify her death certificate. Diagnosing such a cause of death is easy. His report will list her death accurately.

The woman, returning home from a legal abortion, is not reported for the reason stated in the previous question.

Legal abortion complications in the small or private hospital are often not reported for reasons that have nothing to do with protecting the woman but actually are to protect the doctor's reputation. The woman done in a private hospital or clinic who has complications will usually either remain there or go back to the same physician for care. If she dies, that same physician will sign her death certificate. To protect his own reputation as a surgeon he finds it desirable not to report her death as due to the abortion. In fact, this has happened almost routinely in some areas.

In Los Angeles, for instance, in the fall of 1972, stories of three mothers who died following abortions were reported in the newspapers. An inquiring reporter found that one, a healthy 21 year old girl had flown in from Dallas on a Saturday night, was injected with salt, and died Sunday morning. Her death was listed as being from "Spontaneous gangrene of the ovary." When the proper officials were interviewed —

> "Dr. Lester Hibbard, chairman of the L.A. County Medical Society Committee charged with keeping track of maternal deaths, said in an interview that he had official knowledge of only four deaths in the county due to therapeutic abortion since the law was liberalized in November 1967.

> "He said he knows of four additional deaths due to legal abortion, but they were not so reported on the death certificates. Hibbard said he is certain there have been more deaths than these eight but it is not possible to say how many.

> "One reason is that doctors sometimes list a death as due to anaesthesia without making any mention that the patient was pregnant."

> Los Angeles Times, Part II, September 15, 1972

How many actual deaths are there?

In this city, almost accidentally, three deaths were revealed in one month. *Officially* however, there had been only four deaths in the preceding five years.

The thing to remember is that the official U.S. statistics will only report the official four. How many were there really? Perhaps three a month for those 60 months. (180 total)? We think not, but how many? A total of 180 would be 90 times what is actually reported and probably is unrealistic but let's at least assume ten times as many as are being reported.

Now apply these same facts to the New York statistics which claim (reported) only 2-5 deaths for every 100,000 abortions. The actual is then 20-50??

And elsewhere?

The U.S. Bureau of Vital Statistics reported no maternal deaths from induced abortion in Ohio in 1977. In strict confidence your authors were given details of two mothers who had died in Ohio in 1977 from first trimester abortions. They were not and will not be reported because "someone might find out."

I've heard that 8,000 to 20,000 mothers used to die every year from illegal abortions in the U.S.A.

Even the avid pro-abortionist Dr. Christopher Tietze, has called this figure "unmitigated nonsense."

The Bureau of Vital Statistics of the U.S. Public Health Department list the following total number of deaths from abortion, in the entire United States:

in 1942 there were 1232

in 1947 there were 583

in 1957 there were 260

in 1968 there were 130

in 1978 there were 50

Is this accurate?

Perhaps a few can be covered up, but not many. These figures essentially reflect the actual state of affairs. For instance, the Ohio State Medical Association reported that deaths in Ohio from abortions have averaged 6.5 annually over the last decade. Illinois averaged eight annually from 1942-67.

What about legal abortion deaths, do we know anything?

Magee Hospital for Women in Pittsburgh in 1970 had three mothers become desperately ill after legal abortions with one dying in spite of 30 units of blood, and hemodialysis, out of almost 900 abortions. (rate 110/100,000)

Personal Communication

In Maryland, with medical care comparable to that of New York, the abortion mortality rate is 30/100,000.

THERAPEUTIC ABORTION IN MARYLAND IN 1968-70
American Journal of OB & Gyn., June, 1972.

What of New York? Recent figures from there indicate a "remarkable safety record",

Several things are evident when one tries to get an accurate picture of what New York's record is.

a) New York City proper has more stringent regulations and is reporting better than the out-of-city areas. Most reports have come from New York City, not from out of the City. Even Cornell University Medical Center, however, reports that they have completely lost to follow-up 53% of the abortion cases that they have done.

Kings County Hospital Center in Brooklyn performed 6256 abortions in its first year. In their published report it states ". . . *because of the large number of patients aborted and the difficulty of obtaining adequate follow up as the patients returned to their various locales, we could not obtain a satisfactory follow up.*"

IMMEDIATE MORBIDITY ON A LARGE ABORTION SERVICE,
L. Walton, N.Y. State Journal of Med., April 15, 1972.

b) The abortion mills on Long Island and elsewhere frequently don't report at all, and in some cases send 90% or more of their patients back out of state. Usually they do no follow-up at all.

c) Pro-abortionists are extremely defensive and in justifying their activities seem to, at times, be quite selective of the figures that they report.

d) Fantastic profits are being made both as to reported income and unreported income. The abortion "business" is grossing over 100 million dollars annually in greater New York City alone. With this type of money available we should not be surprised that favorable figures are at times the only ones published.

What of other out of New York state deaths?

In Ohio alone in the fall of 1971, there were two deaths, one from New York City (under 12 weeks) and one from Buffalo.

Middletown Journal, Oct. 15, 1971

In 1976 Ohio had a perfect record. No mothers had been reported as dying from induced abortion. Your author knew of two deaths, reported to him only after being sworn to secrecy as to details. They were both 1st trimester suction but listed other causes of death.

Gordon Chase, Pro Abortion Lecturer and N.Y. City Health Commissioner, reported a figure of only 5.3 per 100,000 — what of this?

The Amicus Curiae Brief (p. 87) details that at the very time he reported the above, he completely ignored seven other documented deaths in New York City, plus two others known to have died after returning to their homes, out of state (Mass. and Indiana).

Do the statisticians admit their figures are inaccurate?

No and that is incredible. Ask a health officer what the Gonorrhea incidence is in his or her county and you will be given a figure. Now note that the figure is the reported one but ask again, "How many cases *are* there actually?" The answer will likely be "Oh, we know that only one in five or ten is actually reported. If you want the true incidence, multiply by five or ten."

Since the reason to cover up an abortion is far more impelling than covering up a case of V.D. it should be obvious, as indicated above, that most abortion deaths and injuries are not reported or are reported as something else.

Could it be that their pro-abortion convictions and their need to sell abortion to the American public allows them to continue this thinly veiled dishonesty?

What does the New York State Medical Society say?

New York State Medical Society Guidelines of July 1, 1970, include the statement: *"Abortion performed after the twelfth week is fraught with tremendous danger."*

What does the American College of Obstetrics and Gynecology say about the safety of abortions?

Their official statement in May of 1968 said: *"It is emphasized that the inherent risk of an abortion is not fully appreciated, both by many in the profession, and certainly not by the public."*

Which is safer the suction or the salt poisoning method?

Salt Poisoning abortion is much more dangerous to the mother. Japan abandoned it totally several years ago. T. Wagatsuma of Tokyo reported 25 maternal deaths from salt poisoning abortion.

Am. J. OB-GYN, 93-743, 1965

Most western countries still use it. Some voices are being heard however as for instance:

"Saline Amniocentesis abortion has the highest fatality rate of any elective surgical technique, second only to cardiac transplantation."

N. Kaplan, M.D., J. Am. Med. Assn., p. 89, July 3, '72

The injection of saline also causes a sudden and severe drop in the blood clotting ability of the mother. This *"striking abnormality"* can cause serious internal bleeding and sometimes death.

Dr.'s H. Glueck and A. Weiss, Third Congress of the International Society on Thrombosis and Hemostasis, August 1972

— "Saline-induced abortion is now the first or second most common cause of obstetric hypofibrinogenemia."

DIC more common threat with use of Saline Abortion, L. Talbert, U. of N. Ca., Family Practice News, Vol. 5: No. 19, Oct. 1975

Are blood transfusions a cause of death in abortions?

Yes, very much so, and these deaths never are associated directly, nor reported as statistics related to abortions. Here's how this works:

For every 1,000 units (pints) of blood transfused, one pint will carry a virus that is serious enough to ultimately cause a fatal hepatitis in the person who receives it. Receiving one unit of blood has the same mortality as having your appendix removed. If a woman hemorrhages during an abortion procedure, and many do, she will seldom need only one unit of blood; she will usually need three or four, or even more pints of blood. If we would take four pints as the average number needed for the woman who hemorrhages, then it is evident that of every 250 women transfused, one will die within the next several months of infectious hepatitis. Her death will be listed as being from hepatitis, not abortion.

How many women who have had abortions die as a result of the transfusions needed?

Dr. W. Droegemuller, reporting on the first year experience of Colorado, reported that eight out of every 100 women who were aborted needed blood transfusions.

American Journal of OB and Gyn., Mar. 1969

The English Journal Lancet reports 9% need transfusions. Some have reported much less.

LEGAL ABORTION, A CRITICAL ASSESSMENT OF ITS RISKS,
J. Stallworthy et al., Lancet, Dec. 4, 1971

Certainly a conservative estimate would be 2-3%. If one woman (see above) in every 250 who are transfused ultimately dies of hepatitis, and one woman in every 30-50 who are "done" is transfused, there are ultimately 8 or more who die (per 100,000 abortions) in addition to those reported as abortion deaths.

Are blood clots ever a problem?

Blood clots are one of the causes of death to mothers who deliver babies normally. They are also a cause of death in healthy young women who have abortions performed. In the English study reported below, one out of four mothers who died from abortions did so from blood clots.

Embolism (floating objects in the blood that go to the lungs) is another problem. Childbirth is a normal process, and the body is well prepared for the birth of the child and the separation and expulsion of the placenta. Surgical abortion is an abnormal process, and scrapes the unripe placenta from the wall of the uterus where its roots have grown. This sometimes causes the fluid around the baby, or other pieces of tissue, or blood clots, to be forced into the mother's circulation. These then travel to her lungs, causing damage and occasional death. This is also a major cause of maternal deaths from the salt poisoning method of abortion.

What is the cause of death in mothers who have legal abortions?

In a series of eight maternal abortion deaths. The causes were as follows:

Blood clot in lung	*- two cases*
Anesthetic death	*- one case*
Heart	*- one case*
Cause unknown	*- one case*

> *Complication, illegal abortion*   *- one case*
> *Suicide following legal abortion*   *- two cases*

BRITISH MEDICAL JOURNAL, May 30, 1970, p. 530

How do other countries compare as to abortion vs. child-birth deaths?

According to the documented statistics in an Amicus Curiae Brief, the following is reported:

Country	Maternal Mortality per 100,000 abortions	Maternal Mortality per 100,000 live births
Sweden (up to 20 wks)	39	14.0
Denmark (up to 12 wks)	30	10-20
Hungary (up to 12 wks)	1.2	49.7

U.S. Supreme Court, Roe vs. Wade, and Doe vs. Bolton, Oct. 1971, Horan et al

Official Canadian figures for 1970 listed their abortion mortality at 36 per 100,000 abortions. They shared with the United States Maternal Mortality figures of about 20 per 100,000 live births. (Now about 9.0).

Professor Ian Donald, Professor of Midwifery, Glasgow University, reported on 20,000 legal abortions in England in 1969, which had resulted in the deaths of fifteen mothers. More simply stated, this means that there was almost one death for every 1,000 legal abortions. To say the least, this is an extremely sobering fact, and demonstrates the fallacy of the oft-repeated statement of Dr. Alan Guttmacher, President of Planned Parenthood, that legal abortions are "magnificently safe."

> *"We can look forward to this (legal abortion) being the dominant cause of death to young women."*

THE SCOTSMAN, March 9, 1970

Hungary's figure of 1.2 above seems absurd, is it accurate?

Pro abortionists use the figure constantly citing the "remarkable safety of early abortions". This is a published figure but not an accurate one for three reasons:

a) Under-reporting
b) Abortion deaths possibly listed in maternal figures
c) Censorship by Communist Bureaus prior to publication.

Hungary has some of the most primitive medical care on the continent. The above figures would seem to indicate that it is 25 times safer to abort, but, about four times more dangerous to have a baby than in Denmark. Since all of the more sophisticated medical countries of Europe agree with Denmark and Sweden's figures, no defense of the Hungarian figures is possible.

11

PHYSICAL HARM
FROM ABORTIONS?

Hemorrhage — perforation — infection — prematurity — miscarriage — sterility — menstrual disturbances — tubal pregnancy — synechia — adherent placenta — neonatal death — increased deformities — Rh sensitization — hepatitis.

Are abortion complications accurately reported?

As with deaths, few are reported. For example, the Ohio Dept. of Health in May 1977 reported that "there is no information available as to complications on the abortion procedure. . . ." and further "the reporting on this statistic has been very minimal."

What other bad effects come to the mother from abortion?

One well documented study comes from Charles University in Prague, Czechoslovakia, reporting on thirteen years of carefully done abortions. All were done in the gynecology department of a hospital. The limit was 12 weeks (3 months) of pregnancy. Vacuum curettage was used. The patient stayed on average of 3-5 days in the hospital, one week more at home, and got insurance for lost wages.

"Acute inflammatory conditions occur in 5% of the cases, whereas permanent complications such as chronic inflammatory conditions of the female organs, sterility, and ectopic [tubal] pregnancies are registered in 20-30% of all women ... these are definitely higher in primagravidas [aborted for first pregnancy]". *"Especially striking is an increased incidence in ectopic pregnancies. A high incidence of cervical incompetance resultant from abortion has raised the incidence of spontaneous abortions [miscarriage] to 30-40%. We rather often observe complications such as rigidity of the cervical os, placenta adherens, placenta accreta, and atony of the uterus."*

A. Kodasek, ARTIFICIAL TERMINATION OF PREGNANCY IN CZECHOSLOVAKIA, Int. J. of Gyn. & OB, 1971, Vol. 9, No. 3

Increase in prematurity?

— After one legal abortion the increase of premature births is 14%, after two it is 18%, after three it is 24%.

Klinger, DEMOGRAPHIC CONSEQUENCES OF THE LEGALIZATION OF ABORTION IN EASTERN EUROPE, Int. J. Gyn & OB. 8:691, Sept. 1971

— Non-aborted women have a premature rate of 5%, aborted women a rate of 14%.

R. Slumsky, COURSE OF DELIVERY OF WOMEN FOLLOWING INTERRUPTION OF PREGNANCY, Cesk. Gynek 29;97, 1964

— Women who have had abortions have twice the chance of a premature baby later.

G. Papaevangelou, U. Hosp. Athens Greece
J. OB-GYN Br. Commonwealth 80:418-22, 1973

— In Czechoslovakia premature births resultant from abortions are so frequent that a woman, who has had several abortions, who gets pregnant, is examined and:

"If the physicians can see scar tissue, they will sew the cervix closed in the 12th or 13th

week of pregnancy. The patient stays in the hospital as long as necessary, which in some cases means many months.

Birth injuries from premature births?

With a higher percent of premature birth, the Czechs are also finding a higher percent of brain injuries at birth. Dr. Zedowsky reports on

"A growing number of children requiring special education because of mental deficits related to prematurity."

CZECHS TIGHTEN REINS ON ABORTION
Medical World News, 106J, 106H, 1973

"Prematurity was a direct or contributory cause in over 50% of deaths during the first month of life. The death rate of the premature baby ran about thirty times higher than among full-term infants. If premature infants survive, they face a higher frequency of the tragic aftermath of mental retardation, neurologic diseases and blindness."

THE CHALLENGE OF PREMATURITY
Dennis Cavanaugh, M.D.
Medical World News, Feb. 1971

It is entirely possible, in countries that have abortion on demand, that the number of defective babies killed by abortion will be more than supplanted by a greater number of defective babies, caused by prematurity, which is a direct result of the previous legal abortions of their mothers.

Why this increase in prematurity?

When an abortion is done, the cervical muscle must be stretched open to allow the surgeon to enter the uterus. In a D & C for a spontaneous miscarriage, no harm is done as the cervix is usually soft and often open. Also, there is rarely any damage done by a D & C done on a woman for excessive menstruation, etc. When however, a normal, well rooted placenta and growing baby are scraped out of a firmly closed uterus, protected by a long, "green" cervical muscle, the task of dilating this muscle is more difficult. Undoubtedly some muscle fibers are torn, permanently weakening it. Stanford University Hospital, for example, reported:

> *"In our hospital amongst nulliparous (first pregnancy) patients undergoing suction curratage for therapeutic abortion, about one in eight required suture (stitches) of the cervix because of laceration occurring during the process of dilatation."*

R.C. Goodlin, M.D., OB-Gyn Collected
Letters of the International Correspondence Society
of Obstetricians and Gynecologists, p. 97, June 15, 1971.

This weakening at times results in an "incompetent cervix" which will open prematurely, causing premature birth, as it is not strong enough to hold the heavier weight of a full term child. It is also probably responsible for the increase of later spontaneous miscarriage seen after legal abortions.

It was estimated that hepatis kills eight or more out of every 100,000 mothers who have an abortion. Does hepatitis have harmful effects in others who get the disease but recover?

For every one woman who has hepatitis severe enough to be fatal, there are dozens of women who have milder cases of hepatitis, with resulting lengthy illnesses and often some degree of permanent loss of physical health and stamina.

What about sterility?

Some older women would not mind if they become sterile, but more abortions are done on young ladies who do want to have children in the future. In a cross-section of the general population, about 10% of all marriages will be childless for a wide variety of reasons. If a woman has had one legal abortion, the additional sterility rate reported is up to 10% (Poland 6.9%, Japan 9.7%, with similar results reported from Holland, Norway, Singapore and Russia).

INDUCED ABORTION, A Documented Report,
Hilgers & Shearin, 1971, p. 30

— In 1974, Dr. Bohumil Stipal, Czechoslovakia's Deputy Minister of Health, stated

> *"Roughly 25% of the women who interrupt their first pregnancy have remained permanently childless."*

What of Rh problems?

Induced abortion even in the early weeks can sensitize a mother so that in later pregnancies her babies will have Rh problems, need transfusions, and occasionally be born dead or die after birth. This can be tested for and largely prevented by giving a very expensive medication called Rhogam. Unfortunately, many of the abortion chambers now operating "legally" do not take this expensive precaution.

An increase in tubal pregnancies after a legal abortion?

Yes. The suction and scraping of the inside of the womb, while cutting up and removing the unborn baby, sometimes causes scarring so that later the fertilized egg cannot move normally down and out of the tube to nest in the wall of the womb. The growing new human body (zygote) then nests and starts to grow in the mother's tube. Within a few weeks, this causes an acute abdominal condition in the mother, with internal hemorrhage necessitating an emergency operation and removal of the tube.

Tubal pregnancies in the U.S. constitute 0.5% of all pregnancies but after abortion rise to 3.9%.

Amicus Curiae Brief, U.S. Supreme Court, 1971, Horan et al

What about miscarriage later?

— As a general rule, many now believe that one suction abortion, done on a first pregnancy will double the woman's chances for miscarriages later but, *"There was a tenfold increase in the number of second trimester miscarriages in pregnancies which followed a vaginal abortion."*

Second Trimester Abortion after Vaginal Termination of Pregnancy, Wright, et al, The Lancet, June 10, 1972

— Women who had one induced abortion had a 17.5% miscarriage rate in subsequent pregnancies as compared to a 7.5% rate in a non-aborted group.

Effects of Legal Termination on Subsequent Pregnancy, Richardson & Dickson, Br. Med. J. 1:1303-4, p. 21, 1976

And more babies die during pregnancy and delivery?

The incidence of fetal death during pregnancy and labor is twice normal, if the mother has been aborted previously.

McDonald & Auro, S. Med. J. 67-560-66, 1974

Any effect on subsequent children?

There is *"a growing number of children born prematurely who must attend special schools because they are not as intelligent as their full term peers.*

Vedra, Zidovsky, Med. World News, Oct. 12, 1973

What are some of the other physical problems encountered from abortion?

— Other damage to the mother includes perforation, (1.0% of legal abortions) resulting in peritonitis and occasional death, but more frequently, emergency removal of the uterus.

Amicus Curiae Brief, U.S. Supreme Court, 1971, Horan et al

— Adherent placenta (afterbirth) is another problem. Normally at delivery, the placenta separates easily from the inside of the womb, and is delivered very soon after the baby. In some women who have had induced abortions, the placenta becomes adherent to the inside wall of the uterus, does not separate normally, produces hemorrhage, and sometimes necessitates its surgical removal.

— Synechia or scarring together of the inner walls of the uterus also occurs.

— Fetal hemographs — *"Implanted fetal tissues must be considered when a mass or polyp is seen in a woman with a previous abortion."*

Predicts Highest Abortion Morbidity Yet to Come.
McDonald and Aaro, May Clinic,
Fam. Practice News, Sept. 15, 1974

— Six percent of women who become pregnant after hysterotomy abortions suffered rupture of their uterus. Substantial risk of rupture was demonstrated in 26%. Babies who were born subsequently were small for their due date.

The Wounded Uterus: Pregnancy after Hysterotomy
Clow & Crompton, British Med. J., p. 321, 2-10-73

"Complications are almost certainly under-reported because those treated outside of hospitals are seldom included in hospital statistics."

Jurukoveski and Sukarovsay, Int. J. Gyn. Ob. 9:111-17, 1971

Where can one find full documentation of published reports on abortion complications?

The most important collection of scientific papers detailing damage is the Wynn Report. These (pro-abortion) doctors have published an exhaustive report of physical and mental complications of induced abortion in the United Kingdom and elsewhere.

SOME CONSEQUENCES OF INDUCED ABORTION
TO CHILDREN BORN SUBSEQUENTLY,
Margaret and Arthur Wynn, 1972
Foundation of Education & Research in Child Bearing, London

The Japanese have aborted for over 20 years, what's their record?

— The 1969 Survey of the Office of the Prime Minister of Japan listed the following complaints after abortion:

1) 9% sterility

2) 14% subsequent habitual spontaneous miscarriage

3) 400% increase in tubal pregnancies

4) 17% menstrual irregularities

5) 20-30% abdominal pain, dizziness, headaches, etc.

These complications make it sound like abortion is more dangerous than delivering a baby. That's not what I've been reading.

The above figures speak for themselves. Many people who are in favor of abortion are honest and well-intentioned. Unfortunately, a great many of those favoring abortion simply do not know the facts, choose to ignore them, or brush over them in their eagerness to convince our society that destroying unborn human lives would solve many of our problems. If we actually compare similar age groups of women who have had induced abortions and women who have delivered babies, we find that it is much more damaging to their physical health to have an abortion.

"There has been almost a conspiracy of silence in declaring its risks. Unfortunately, because of emotional reactions to legal abortion, well-documented evidence from countries with a vast experience of it receives little attention in either the medical or lay press. This is medically indefensible when patients suffer as a result. For these reasons, we summarize the facts of our experience in

*this division of Obstetrics and Gynecology.
We are proud neither of the number of pregnancies which have been terminated nor the
complications described."*

In the experience of this English-teaching
hospital there was a 27% complication rate
from infection, 9.5% needed transfusions, 5%
of suction and D&C abortions tore the cervical muscle, and 1.7% perforated. *"It is significant that some of the more serious complications occurred with the most senior and
experienced operators."*

These complications . . . *"are seldom mentioned by those who claim that abortion is
safe . . . "*

LEGAL ABORTION, A CRITICAL ASSESSMENT OF ITS RISKS,
J.A. Stallworthy at al, The Lancet, December 4, 1971

12

PRIVATE ABORTION CHAMBERS

The U.S. Supreme Court has said that it is legal to kill unborn babies. We cannot protect their lives at this time. The least we can do is to protect the lives and health of the unfortunate women who do decide to kill their babies. What is needed in each city or state is a set of medically sound regulations that would at least partly keep the new private, abortion chambers from exploiting the women they claim to help! Why is regulation needed? Let's compare!

Legitimate Surgical Practice	Commercial Abortion Chambers
Kickbacks	
If a legitimate surgeon gave kickbacks, he would lose his surgical privileges and perhaps his license too.	Kickbacks from surgeons or clinics are common, e.g., Planned Parenthood-Clergy Counseling Service of Los Angeles in 1972 received $250,-000.00 from the clinics and private "hospitals" to whom they referred women for abortions. (L.A. Free Press, 9-15-72)

Legitimate Surgical Practice	Commercial Abortion Chambers

Pathological Exam

Pathological specimens are routinely examined by a licensed pathologist, and a permanent record made.

Pathological specimens (the pieces of the baby and his placenta) are seldom so examined.

Cash-at-the-Door

If a surgeon routinely requied cash at the door this unethical action would probably cause him to lose his surgical privileges.

Cash at the door on admission is routine. A few are "done" free for window dressing, but for the average woman it's cash or no abortion.

Advertising

If a surgeon were to advertise in a paper, on radio, or by mail, etc. he would lose his license.

Advertising is routine.

Counseling

Considering the possible permanent psychic and physical consequences, no conscientious physician would do an operation without fully explaining to the mother any and all possibilities of complications at the time of surgery and in future years.

Most abortion "counseling" can best be described as a farce. To our knowledge, there is not a single abortion chamber, Clergy Counseling, or Planned Parenthood service that will tell, *and show in pictures,* the stage of development of her baby, nor do they tell of possible complications to her and to her babies later.

Laws should require that a Planned Parenthood type *and* a Birthright or Right to Life type coun-

Legitimate Surgical Practice	Commercial Abortion Chambers
	selor both see the mother and sign on the operative permit that she has been fully informed of both sides of the issue.

Blood Transfusions

Legitimate Surgical Practice	Commercial Abortion Chambers
A legitimate surgical service will have blood transfusion services readily available.	In spite of the fact that from 2% to 12% women having these "safe" suction abortions bleed so badly that they need transfusions, it is rare to have such service quickly available.

Rh Sensitization

Legitimate Surgical Practice	Commercial Abortion Chambers
It is well known that Rh sensitization can occur from a suction abortion. A hospital will always test for it and if indicated give the expensive Rhogam which will prevent sensitization.	It is estimated that less than half of profit making abortion chambers test for the Rh factor and use Rhogam. The result of this abuse is that some of these women can't have babies later because of this sensitization.

Surgeon's Income

Legitimate Surgical Practice	Commercial Abortion Chambers
The average surgeon in the USA has an annual income of about $60,000.00	It is not unusual for an abortion doctor, working full time to make $250,-000.00 a year.

Record Keeping

Legitimate Surgical Practice	Commercial Abortion Chambers
In a hospital, permanent detailed records are kept of what is done and of complications.	Abortion chamber's record keeping vary from brief to almost non-existant. It is the scandal of our nation that abortion

Legitimate Surgical Practice	Commercial Abortion Chambers
	complications (and deaths) are commonly not reported. (see chapter 10).

Follow up Care

Legitimate surgical care mandates a follow up exam a few weeks post-operative.	Profit making abortion chambers almost never do any follow up. The woman leaves and is on her own.

Correct Diagnosis

No legitimate surgeon would operate until a definite diagnosis were made. If in doubt, an ethical surgeon would ask for consultation from colleagues.	In some abortion chambers as many as 10% of the women "aborted" are not pregnant. One New York woman committed suicide from remorse after being aborted (exam revealed she had not been pregnant when "aborted").

Husband, Parents Consent

If a wife needs surgery, (except in dire emergency) no ethical surgeon would operate without consulting with the husband. No minor girl would be touched either without the consent and/or knowledge of her parents.	Abortion chambers do not inform the husband. In most areas they do not inform or ask consent of parents.

Tissue Disposal

In a hospital, human tissue is disposed of in a dignified manner.	In abortion chambers, human tissue is usually treated like garbage.

Legitimate Surgical Practice	Commercial Abortion Chambers
Burial	
In a hospital the body of a dead person is carefully handled, respected and given to the care of a funeral director.	The bodies of babies killed by abortion end up in the garbage can or down the garbage disposal unit.
Surgical Training	
No surgeon is allowed to operate in a hospital unless he has had lengthy surgical training and been judged competent.	In an abortion chamber, any "licensed physician" can do abortions whether he is a surgeon or not. (illegal abortion has simply been legalized).
Length of Hospital Stay	
A woman who has a D&C in a hospital is usually hospitalized at least two days.	In profit making abortion chambers, she may be sent home only a few hours after the procedure.
Non-Medical Reasons	
With the exception of certain cosmetic plastic surgery, all surgery is done for medical reasons.	About 98% of abortions are done for social, not medical reasons.
Insurance-Elective Surgery	
Medicaid and other insurances do not cover elective surgery such as cosmetic plastic surgery.	Strangely, in most states, insurance does cover induced abortion, 98% of which are done for elective, non-medical reasons.

Legitimate Surgical Practice	Commercial Abortion Chambers

Discipline Surgeons

If a surgeon continued to get serious complications from his mishandling of his cases of appendicitis, he would be examined by his colleagues and his right to operate possibly withdrawn.	If a physician has too many complications resulting from the abortions he has done, there is no way to stop him.

To allow the killing of babies prior to birth at the mother's request by a death technician, the doctor, is a tragic thing. The U.S. Supreme Court has legalized this killing.

Our total intention in relating the above is to call attention to the ruthless exploitation of women that is now occurring. The woman who comes for abortion is often alone and away from the support of her loved ones. She is making a decision that she will carry on her conscience the rest of her life. The abortion itself can result in permanent physical and psychic after effects. Because of this at least she must have full factual information upon which to base her decision. The decision, is legally her's to make. Because of this, she deserves at least reasonable medical and surgical care. This she commonly does not get.

Why? Dr. Mildred Jefferson, the first black woman graduate of Harvard Medical College and a teaching surgeon at Boston University recently gave her answer: "After all, they're only women!"

13

REDUCE ILLEGAL ABORTION?

"Women should not be subjected to back room kitchen-table butchery. Thousands of married women as well as single girls die every year because the law has driven them to attic hideouts and motel room surgery."

Ann Landers
The Cincinnati Post & Times-Star
December 23, 1969

Who would argue?

No one would defend the crude abortion done by an unqualified person in unsterile surroundings. The above argument is a very powerful one, and has been used with telling effect on legislators throughout the world. If it were true, it would be a very strong argument indeed in favor of at least some legalization of abortion. The problem is that our esteemed columnist has been misinformed, and so has most of the world. Her concern is shared by us all but, legalizing abortion does not, has not, and apparently will not reduce the number of self induced or back street abortions.

What is the difference between illegal abortion and back-street abortion?

People usually confuse the two. Illegal abortions are those carried out by a doctor but against the law. Back-street abortion is that carried out by an unqualified person. Naturally, being unreported, no one can ever know the numbers. A New York Planned Parenthood official however, estimated that before legalization, between 80 and 90% of illegal abortions were done by doctors, probably the same ones who are now doing them legally.

England has had a very permissive law since 1967. Illegal abortions have certainly decreased there, haven't they?

— *"There has certainly been no decrease in the number of back street abortion dealt with by us since 1967."*

> J.C. McClure Brown, Hamersmith Hosp. London
> The London Evening News, April 18, 1974

— The United Bristol Hospitals reported:

"It seems likely that there has been a rise in the number of criminal abortions in Bristol since the Abortion Act." Further that the legalization of abortion *"has either engendered a less responsible attitude to contraception or there has been an actual increase in the number of promiscuous pregnancies in unmarried women."*

> A.H. John & B. Hackman, EFFECTS OF
> LEGAL ABORTION ON GYNECOLOGY,
> British Medical Journal, 1972, 3, 99-102

— *"It appears that increasing number of women are turning to back street abortionists."*

> H. Graham, Pregnancy Advisory Service,
> London Evening News, April 18, 1974

— The most authoritative report on this was published by the Royal College of Obstetrics and Gynecology, and constituted a summary of the opinions of the Consultant Obstetricians of England. It said:

> "The original protagonists for abortion law reform often argued that a large proportion of cases of spontaneous abortions hitherto treated in hospitals and nearly all the associated deaths were the result of criminal interference. Legalization of abortion would, they postulated, eliminate these. They brushed aside contrary arguments and evidence. Our figures show . . . that despite a sharp rise in the number of therapeutic ('legal') abortions from 1968 to 1969, there was not, unfortunately, a significant change in the number of cases of spontaneous [criminal] abortion requiring admission to hospital.

> "The fact that legalization of abortion has not so far materially reduced the numbers of spontaneous abortions or of deaths from abortions of all kinds is not surprising. It confirms the experience of most countries and was forecast by the College's 1966 statement."

> British Med. Journal, May 1970

How about Sweden? Hasn't it reduced illegal abortions there?

No, it hasn't. Sweden is generally considered to have one of the more "enlightened and progressive laws." The prestigious British Medical Journal Lancet; stated *"Sweden's law, in its present form, has not sufficed to subdue criminal abortion."*

ON THE OUTCOME OF PREGNANCY WHEN LEGAL ABORTION IS READILY AVAILABLE, The Lancet, Mar. 2, 1968, p. 467.

Dr. Christopher Tietze, a well known pro-abortion biostatistician has written:

> "One of the major goals of the liberalization of abortion laws in Scandanavia was to reduce the in-

cidence of illegal abortion . . . It is doubtful whether [this objective] has been achieved in any of the countries concerned . . . "

ABORTION IN EUROPE, *Am. Journal of Public Health*, Nov. 1967

What about Germany and Italy?

Pro-abortionists in Germany were claiming that over 15,000 women were dying annually from the more than one million illegal abortions being done in that country. After a thorough investigation by the German Medical Association, it was found that in fact there were fewer than 75,000 illegal abortions being done with an average of 30 deaths annually.

Pro-abortionists are now reporting the 15,000 figure for Italy. In both cases, this is a larger number of women than the total who die annually in either country in the age group of 12-50 years.

Was this also true of Japan?

Even more so in Japan. Of the 50,000,000 unborn children that have been killed by abortions in the last 2 decades in Japan, and where abortions are very inexpensive, perhaps one-half of the procedures continue to be done illegally. *"One million registered abortions suggests two million actual cases of abortion."*

FAMILY PLANNING IN JAPAN: A RECORD OF FAILURE, Asahi Journal, Oct. 16, 1966, p. 52

What of East Germany, Switzerland, Russia, Poland and other countries?

Drs. Hilgers and Shearin from the Mayo Clinic assembled twenty-one scientific reports from ten different countries. Passage of permissive abortion laws had "no effect" on the criminal abortion rate in eight of them. In two countries, it actually increased with liberal abortion law."

INDUCED ABORTION, A DOCUMENTED REPORT, chap. 7, 2nd Edition, January 1973

What of other Iron Curtain Countries?

Rumania has changed its laws from abortion-on-demand back to very rigid restrictions. At an international meeting of Psychosomatic Medicine in Obstetrics and Gynecology, a speaker from Rumania said that despite all warnings that they should not change back the most outstanding factors to emerge during the five years since the change were:

> *"Our men have regained respect for our women. Our women have regained their lost respect for themselves and there has been no increase in back street abortions."*

Nursing Times, London, 1971

> *In Hungary, a few years ago, after 20 years of abortion on demand (1.4 abortions for every live birth), and before the laws were drastically tightened up, infection, due to back street abortions remained one of the major causes of maternal mortality.*

International J. of OB & Gyn., May, 1971

What is the reason why illegal abortions are not reduced?

Here are some examples:

1) Suppose you are the wife of a man who wants another child. You do not. You become pregnant. If you go through official procedures in a hospital, your husband may find out. You don't want him to know, but you want to get rid of this baby, so you have an illegal abortion.

2) Suppose you are a married woman, and you become pregnant by another man. Your hus-

band has been away, and he knows this would not be his child. Again, he must never know that you've become pregnant, so you have it done illegally.

3) Suppose you are a prominent citizen, and your teenage daughter becomes pregnant. You wish to avoid scandal. Hospital procedures are available to her. You cannot, however, take the risk of disclosure. You have it done in the privacy of an illegal situation.

4) Suppose you are poor. Perhaps your man has left you. There is a long waiting list at the public hospital, and much red tape you don't understand. You are frantic to "get rid of it." A friend tells you of someone who will. You go there.

All of the above tell the same story: fear of disclosure, of someone finding out, or of ignorance. In order to make abortions as safe as it is possible to make them, there must be official and scientific supervision, rules, and public inspection. Whether privacy would be violated or not is beside the point. People universally fear that it might, and so, no matter how available legal abortions may be made, people in large numbers will continue to seek illegal ones and suffer the consequences.

But illegal abortions have dropped in New York, haven't they?

The number of admissions for "incomplete" abortions has decreased and therefore it is claimed that illegal abortions have declined — but —

1) Many of these are from spontaneous miscarriages.

2) The total birth rate (and total pregnancies) is sharply down and therefore a similar percent drop in miscarriages should be expected. This accounts for a significant part of the decrease.

3) These reports are from 15 New York City municipal hospitals where the number of legal abortions is so high (2.3 for every live birth at Bellevue Hospital) that admissions for "incompletes" certainly should drop. To accomplish this by what almost amounts to genocide is a staggering price to pay.

4) "It is certain that more women are now dying of abortion in N.Y. City than before the enactment of abortion-on-demand and that the majority of these deaths have been from legal abortions, not illegal."

5) Thousands of N.Y. abortions have been done illegally beyond the 24 week limit. These are illegal or criminal abortions by any standards.

INDUCED ABORTION, A DOCUMENTED REPORT
T. Hilgers, 2nd Edition, January 1973,
Chapter 7

But since you cannot stop illegal abortions why not legalize them?

Since when do we eliminate evil by saying it is good. Did you know that 1,000,000 cars were stolen in the U.S. last year? Surely this can't be stopped. Therefore, why not make it legal to steal cars?

14

PRE-NATAL

AND

POST-NATAL EUTHANASIA

No doctor who kills his patients has ever made a contribution to medicine.

Prof. Jerome Lejeune, Paris

Euthanasia is when the doctor kills the patient.

All of the reasons discussed so far, that have been put forward as justification for abortion, have been so-called maternal indications. They have related directly to the mother, her life, her health, her social or economic well-being, her convenience. In all of them, the physical intactness and perfection, or otherwise, of the growing child within her has not been considered. The consideration has been whether she has wanted to bear a child at all. When considering abortion for fetal defect, we are only peripherally thinking of the mother, who might well sustain certain anguish if she bears such a child. Rather, we are thinking primarily of the child himself, and are asking whether this child has an intact enough mind and body to justify his continued life.

With this thinking we enter an entirely new rationale for justification of the existence of a life. In this case the price tag on the life of this living human, the justification for allowing him to continue to live, is whether or not he will prove independent enough, intelligent enough, and useful enough to society to allow him to live. We cannot emphasize strongly enough that this is an entirely different set of criteria than maternal indications for abortion. It introduces an entirely new set of values into our western civilization's regard for human life, born or unborn.

What do you mean "born or unborn?"

Just that! If one does an abortion because the unborn is handicapped, why is he killing? *Because this living human is not perfect enough.* That is the reason.

He won't discover them all before birth. He'll kill a few normal babies and miss a few "bad" ones. Some will be born. Then he will hold a handicapped infant in his arms. Now remember why he was going to kill this child. Because the child is handicapped! Well, the baby is still handicapped, now he has an exact diagnosis. He meant to kill for the specific reason of handicap didn't he? The baby has merely left the womb. Why does he not go ahead and kill now! That's what he meant to do didn't he? What difference does place of residence make?

Now hold it! I know people who would agree with aborting a handicapped child but wouldn't kill a born one!

Why not? When human life before birth can be destroyed because it will not be a useful and productive life, and that becomes law of the land, there is no logic or rational line to draw between the killing of pre-born children because they're handicapped, and the killing of a post-born child because he is handicapped. This is called infanticide or newborn euthanasia, as opposed to abortion which (if done for defect) is correctly called prenatal euthanasia. Once a policy and an acceptance of euthanasia for a handicapped human life has been established at one stage in human life, then it will be easy to accept euthanasia at other stages of human life as well.

That would be terrible.

But utterly logical! That is the frightening thing about abortion for handicap. The most direct statement on this was by Nobel Laureate James Watson, the man who cracked the genetic code;

> *"Because of the present limits of such detection methods, most birth defects are not discovered until birth.*
>
> *If a child were not declared alive until three days after birth, then all parents could be allowed the choice . . . the doctor could allow the child to die if the parents so choose and save a lot of misery and suffering."*
>
> AMA Prism, Children from the Laboratory,
> May, 1973

— Some of his collegues disagree. Three days is too soon, they would prefer thirty-days after birth.

— The pro-abortionist, Joseph Fletcher, would use the I.Q. measurement and allow those under 20? or perhaps 40 to be declared non-human [who will bid 60?].

— There are some who think that just being black would be reason enough, or perhaps Jews might be declared "non-persons" again.

— Miss Barbara Smoker, President of the National Secular Society, and Vice-Chairman of the British Humanist Association wrote, *"The situation of a newborn baby is very different to that of the same baby, even a few weeks later . . . At birth the baby is only a potential human being and at that point it is surely the humane and sensible thing that the life of any baby with obvious severe defects, whether of body or brain, should be quietly snuffed out by the doctor or midwife. This should not be a decision referred to the family who are too emotionally involved; though in borderline cases the doctor's knowledge of the family situation would be one of the factors taken into account."*

The Times
January 22, 1973

But what of a child with Tay-Sacs Disease, that child will surely die a slow death of deterioration!

So the new "ethic" says that you should kill him early and efficiently! Does age (younger) and place of residence (in the womb) really change what you are doing (killing)? There are dozens of incurable illnesses, some just last longer.

Once you start, where do you stop?

A few Pediatricians in 1939 in Germany began to "terminate" a few idiot children. They were pure blood Aryans but defective. By 1945, these same doctors, in university hospitals had so lowered the price tag that they were killing bed wetters, children with mishapen ears and those with learning disabilities.

The German Euthanasia Program
Wertham, Hayes Pub. Co., 1977, p. 47

The German doctors only did what Hitler ordered, didn't they?

No! The euthanasia program to "purify" the German race was a creation of physicians. The first gas chamber was designed by Professors of Psychiatry from twelve major German universities. They selected the patients and watched them die. They then slowly reduced the "price tag" until the mental hospitals were almost empty.

They were joined by Pediatricians who began by emptying the institutions for defective children, and ended killing bed wetters.

Internists helped empty the homes for the aged. Then some doctors went out into the community. Many defective or old people were taken from their homes and killed. By 1945 the doctors had even eliminated many World War I amputee veterans.

Few know that doctors participating in the "German Euthanasia Program" did so voluntarily. Some left the program and were not retaliated against. Hitler approved and exerted certain pressures but the doctors did it.

Hitler, taking his cue from the physicians, used their gas chambers and proceeded to eliminate "defective" races. He destroyed an entire race of Gypsies, six million Jews, and perhaps almost as many captured Poles, Russians, central Europeans, etc.

The German Euthanasia Program
Wertham, Hayes Pub. Co., 1978

That's unbelievable but how did this relate to abortion?

Although never legalized, abortion had become in fact the accepted answer for the mother's social problem in the 1920's and 30's in Germany. The conscience of the people had become dull. The above physicians, accustomed to accepting the killing of one group of humans who were socially burdensome (the unborn), were apparently able to move logically to killing other classes of humans who were also socially burdensome.

Were all German Doctors quilty?

Certainly not, only about 300 actually did the killing. Over 50,000 did not participate. The major difference from today was that Germany was a dictatorship and it was during a war. Few people really knew many details, fewer still were involved, and little could be done about it.

Today we have an open society and full access to information. If today a nation condones killing for defect (unborn or born) its guilt is immensely greater.

But no one in America would want a "Master Race".

Is there that much difference between the concept of a "Master Race" (quality race) and the "quality life" of our modern pro-abortionist social planners?

> "*The fact that Germany had descended to the depths of Hitlerian mass murders does not immunize you [the U.S.A.] from the same human depravity.*"

Heinrich Pompey, M.D.
Professor, University of Wurtzburg.
Int'nl. Cath. Physician's Guild Meeting
Washington, D.C., October 1970

How could this start here?

First — "*there is a prevalence of thinking in destructive rather than ameliorative terms in dealing with social problems. The ease with which destruction of life is advocated for those considered either socially useless or socially disturbing instead of educational and ameliorative measures may be the first danger sign of loss of creative liberty in thinking which is the hallmark of a democratic society.*"

"*The beginnings [in Germany] were merely a subtle shift in emphasis in the basic attitudes of physicians. It started with the acceptance of the attitude, basic in the euthanasia movement, that there is such a thing as a life not worth living. This attitude in its early stages concerned itself merely with the severely and chronically sick. Gradually, the sphere of those to be included in this catagory was enlarged to include the socially unproductive, the ideologically unwanted, the racially unwanted and finally all non-Germans.*"

"*From the attitude of easing patients with chronic diseases away from the doors of the best types of treatment facilities available to the actual dispatching of such patients to killing centers is a long but nevertheless logical step.*"

Leo Alexander, MEDICAL SCIENCE UNDER DICTATORSHIP,
New England J. of Med., July 1949

What do parents of retarded children think?

"There has not been a single organization of parents of mentally retarded children that has ever endorsed abortion. We, who are parents of these children and have borne the burden, ask that before you, the legislators, propose to speak for us, by possibly authorizing abortion for fetal abnormality, please ask our opinion first."

Mrs. Rosalie Craig, Testimony, Ohio Legislature, 1971

It is of considerable interest that an unusual number of natural and adoptive parents of handicapped children are to be found among the pro-life activists in all countries.

Since most of "nature's mistakes" end in miscarriage doesn't such eugenic abortion merely correct the oversight of nature?

Even if chromosomal studies were routinely done and all such handicapped babies aborted, what would happen when a test might be in error and a handicapped child would "slip through" to be born? That child would still be one of "nature's mistakes". Shouldn't one then follow the logical course and kill that child after birth? If not after, why before birth?

What of Rubella and Its Resultant Handicaps?

Mothers must have Rubella during their first 12 weeks of pregnancy to have their babies affected. However, Dr. Moloshok reviewing fifteen major studies found that only 16.9% of the babies would have defects, and as noted below most are not severe. What this says is that abortion for Rubella will kill 5 normal babies for every defective one. (Why not wait till delivery and then kill the defective one, it would be safer for the mother?)

Moloshok, R.E., FETAL CONSIDERATIONS FOR
THERAPEUTIC ABORTION & STERILIZATION,
Clinical Obstet. Gynec 7:82-99, 1964

What defects come from Rubella?

Of the 16.9% of children who are affected

a) 50% had hearing loss, most correctable by hearing aids

b) 50% had heart defect, almost all surgically correctable

c) 30% had cataracts, often one sided, most had fair vision

d) Mental retardation was 1.5% compared to 1% in a nonaffected population

(Rendle-Short, Lancet 2:373, 1964)

What if a woman receives Rubella vaccine while pregnant?

— There are no reported cases of significant damage to the babies who were born after such vaccination, e.g., *"none of the live born infants had serologic or clinical evidence of congenital rubella."*

S. Wyall, K. Herrmann, INADVERTANT
RUBELLA VACCINATION OF PREGNANT WOMEN,
J. Am. Med. Assn. 225:1472, 1973

— Risk of "infection" of the fetus is "probably less than 5 to 10%." None of the infants born to such vaccinated women had any defects. (They still think she should consider abortion however).

Risk of Congenital Abnormality after Inadvertent
Rubella Vaccination of Pregnant Women
N. Eng. J. Med. 294:972-74, April 29, 1976

But wouldn't care of the handicapped be very costly?

What is your ethic? Do you treat, care for, and help a sick or disabled person, or do you kill him? Do you measure the value of a person's life in money? in utilitarian usefulness?

But isn't it cruel to allow a handicapped child to be born — to a miserable life?

The assumption that handicapped people enjoy life less than "normal" ones has recently been shown to be false. A well documented investigation has shown that there is no difference between handicapped and normal persons in their degree of life satisfaction, outlook of what lies immediately ahead and vulnerability to frustration. *"Though it may be both common and fashionable to believe that the malformed enjoys life less than normal, this appears to lack both empirical and theoretical support."*

Happiness and Life Satisfaction of the Malformed, Proceedings, Am. Psychologic Assn. Meeting 1971, P. Cameron, U. of Louisville, Van Hoeck et al Wayne State U.

You are equating abortion with euthanasia?

That's right. They both directly kill living humans. They both are done for the same reasons.

REASON	ABORTION	EUTHANASIA
Usefulness	a burden	a burden
Wanted	unwanted	unwanted
Degree of Perfection	handicapped	handicapped
Age	too young	too old
Intelligence	not yet conscious	not really conscious any more
Place of residence	in the womb	in institution
"Meaningful life"	"does not yet have" Row v Wade	"no longer has" euthanasia bills

119

But there are different kinds of euthanasia such as active and passive, direct and indirect, voluntary and involuntary, etc.?

Let's clear up this semantic confusion. All of these qualifications are either the product of confused minds, or a direct attempt to change the meaning of the word euthanasia so that we can accept it.

Euthanasia is when the doctor kills the patient.

But I don't want the doctor keeping me alive artificially. Why not a law to permit death with dignity?

No new laws are needed. No doctor in the U.S. has ever been indicted for *allowing* a patient to die a natural death. When a patient is surely dying, doctors may and must use their best judgment as to when and if to continue or to discontinue certain therapeutic efforts that have failed to cure the patient, and which may only be serving to postpone dying. The doctor's only obligation then is keep the patient comfortable and allow a peaceful death.

Doctors have the confidence of patients because their total effort has been to cure. If once medicine moves into the realm of exterminative medicine and doctors begin to kill, then that absolutely essential factor in the doctor-patient relationship, complete confidence, will be destroyed.

But a law to allow "Death with Dignity" would not permit euthanasia.

> *"I imagine our mercy killing laws will begin by legalizing death with dignity,"* but *"next I see these laws being expanded to accomplish the real goal, to get rid of people who are a burden on society."*
>
> Dr. Lois Lobb, The Mercy Killers by Paul Marx

Could you give any recent examples?

In England, only six months after their permissive abortion bill passed, a euthanasia bill narrowly missed passage.

Thirty states in the U.S. have had euthanasia bills introduced.

Dr. Sackett in Florida has stated that 90% of the patients in that state's hospitals for the mentally retarded should be "allowed to die."

The Florida Times Union, January 11, 1973

In 1973 Senator Halleck of Oregon introduced a bill to permit the *"administration of euthanasia"* (defined as *"the painless inducement of death"*) for certain *"unremediable conditions,"* which means:

a) *A serious physical illness which is diagnosed as incurable and terminal, and which is expected to cause a person severe distress, or to render him incapable of a rational existance, or*

b) *"A condition of brain damage or deterioration such that a person's normal mental faculties are severely and irreparably impaired to such an extent that he has been rendered incapable of leading a rational existance."*

Oregon Senate Bill 179, 1973

He, incidentally, had sponsored their abortion bill in 1969.

Before his death Dr. Alan Guttmacher, head of Planned Parenthood World Population was on the Board of the Euthanasia Society of America.

Where does the ACLU stand?

The American Civil Liberties Union's Board of Directors in 1977 states "Consensual euthanasia involves an act or an omission by a second person, at the request of an individual for the termination of the latter's life when he or she is either terminally ill or totally and permanently disabled. The ACLU recognizes this form of euthanasia as a legitimate extension of the right of control over one's own body."

Euthanasia News, Vol. 3, No. 1, Feb. 1977

Any Court Decisions?

One case that will not be forgotten came before the New Jersey Supreme Court in 1967. The parents had sued because the doctor had refused the mother an abortion after she had contracted rubella early in her pregnancy. Their suit was filed after the child had been born deformed. The court said:

> *It is basic to the human condition to seek life and to hold on to it, however burdened. If Jeffrey could have been asked as to whether his life should be snuffed out before his full term of gestation could run its course, our felt intuition of human nature tells us he would almost surely choose life with defects as against no life at all.*

> *'The right of life is unalienable in our society. A court cannot say what defects should prevent an embryo from being allowed life, such that denial of the opportunity to terminate the existence of the defective child in embryo can support a cause of action. The examples of famous persons who have had great achievements despite physical defects come readily to mind, and many of us can think of examples close to home. A child need not be perfect to have a worthwhile life.*

> *"We are not faced with the necessity of balancing the mother's life against that of her child. The sanctity of the single human life is the decisive factor in this suit. Eugenic considerations are not controlling. We are not talking here about the breeding of prize cattle. It may have been easier for the mother, and less expensive for the father, to have terminated the life of their child while he was*

an embryo, but these detriments cannot stand against the preciousness of the single human life."

Gleitman vs. Cosgrove, 1967,
New Jersey Supreme Court

Is there an answer?

The real answer to euthanasia is loving, competent care for the dying. A magnificent new concept for the dying has arisen in England where over 30 institutions called Hospices specialize in compassionate skilled care of the dying.

"Once a patient feels welcome and not a burden to others, once his pain is controlled and other symptoms have been at least reduced to manageable proportions, then the cry for euthanasia disappears. It is not that the question of euthanasia is right or wrong, desirable or repugnant, practical or unworkable. It is just that it is irrelevant. Proper care is the alternative to it, and can be made universally available as soon as there is adequate instruction of medical students in a teaching hospital. If we fail in this duty to care, let us not turn to the politicians asking them to extricate us from this mess."

CARE OF THE DYING, R. Lamerton,
Priory Press Ltd., Pg. 99

15

WHERE WILL IT END

Mark and Julie Welterman sat nervously in State Sanitorium #342 waiting room. A handsome blonde receptionist went about her work, oblivious of their anxieties. The sun's rays pierced the multi-colored skylights and gave an air of majestic awe to the spacious 21st century office.

Mark's hands were cold and clammy as he clutched Julie's tiny hands in his. Beads of perspiration were clearly visible on his slightly wrinkled forehead. And his coarse, wavy hair had lost most of its brilliance. He peered intently at Julie, whose eyes were glued to the glistening marble floor. She's still as beautiful as she was when we courted, 30 years ago, Mark thought. She still has that olive soft skin, the long shimmering black hair, those big brown eyes and little turned up nose and those soft red lips that never uttered an unkind word. How could I have been so lucky, he thought, and now to be put through this. It just isn't right. His thoughts were broken by a husky voice from a young man in white, "Mrs. Welterman."

"Ye-yes?" Julie's voice trembled. "We have completed our findings concerning your mother." Julie tried to speak but nothing came out; only her lips moved. Finally Mark asked, "What was the decision?"

"She is ready to be eliminated," came the cold, matter-of-fact answer. Julie went limp and sobbed bitterly in Mark's arms. "But there must be some mistake," Mark pleaded. "There's nothing wrong with Julie's mother. She's more spry than a lot of the others and not nearly as old as most."

"You know the decision of the board is final. They report that Mrs. Welterman is becoming senile. She forgets things. She can no longer converse intelligently, and her productive output has dropped to the point that it is no longer economically feasible to maintain her."

"It still isn't right. She has been a good subject and the State knows this. I think she deserves some consideration." "Are you questioning the State's authority?" "Oh, no sir. I just hoped that it wouldn't be so soon. As you can see, my wife isn't prepared." "Do you wish to submit your request to the board?" "We would like to." "All right. Step this way."

Mark helped Julie to her feet and they proceeded through a pale blue and orange, diamond shaped door that slid open electronically. Three men dressed in white sat behind a long elevated desk. The middle man seemed to be in charge. He rose. "Come in. Come in and be seated." He waved to two chairs in front of, but about five feet below the elevation of the board members' desk. "You have a question?" Mark leaned forward in his chair. "I have a request sir." "And what is the request?"

"Well, as you can see, my wife's extremely overwrought. We had no idea that her mother's termination would be this soon." "Simpson, didn't you explain the situation to Mr. and Mrs. Welterman?" "I did sir, but they wanted to pursue it further." "Am I to understand that you want us to make an exception in your case and order a postponement?" "Yes sir."

"Do you realize that if the board make an exception in your case then others would have requests, and this would lead to still more. Eventually we would lose control, with no respect for authority. We would end up with mass confusion. You do understand?" "Yes sir." "You are aware of course, that there is no pain connected to it." "No pain at all?" "None whatsoever." The man in charge stood again, signalling an end to the meeting. "If you wish to observe, Simpson will take you to the termination chamber.

Mark's legs barely held his weight as he and Julie tried to rise. His head was spinning as he moved trancelike behind the attendant. They entered a narrow room that seemed to be miles long. He shivered uncontrollably from the uncanny chill inside. A glass partition separated one side from the other. The wall on their side was lined with chairs where somber couples sat stoney-faced. The other side was equipped with special tables. Attendants brought old people in and secured them to the tables. A man in white took a hypodermic needle from a nurse's tray. He extracted fluid from a corked container and injected an old lady. A timer over the table ticked off five seconds, the attendant pulled a sheet over her head and her body was wheeled out of the room.

Two attendants brought in Julie's mother. Her face was a picture of terror as she saw Julie and Mark. Mark could make out the words. "Help me, help me," coming from her trembling lips. As Mark watched the fluid being drawn from its container his eyes blurred and his head started spinning. He slumped unconsciously to the floor. Julie dropped to the floor and shook him vigorously. Her voice was like a whisper in the distance. "Mark, Mark, wake up. What's wrong Mark?"

He tried to move his arms, his legs, his fingers, but couldn't. He seemed completely paralyzed. Julie's words became clearer. He felt himself being shaken. He opened his eyes.

"Mark, honey, wake up. What's wrong?" "Oh, darling, I had the most horrible dream." He held her very close. "I gather as much from the way you were moaning." "Where's your mother?" he asked, pushing her away.

"She's out in the kitchen. We were talking. She was saying how terrible it is that abortion is now legal. You heard about the Supreme Court ruling, didn't you?" "Yes. I was reading about it just before I dozed off."

"I wonder what it will all lead to," Julie said as she disappeared into the kitchen.

Arnold R. Smith

16

FETAL EXPERIMENTATION

What is fetal experimentation?

Experimentation can be carried out on the living human fetus while he or she still lives in the womb. Experimentation can be carried out on the living human baby after delivery. If the experiment is done for the possible benefit of this specific living human (e.g. trial of a drug in treatment) then it is ethical if the parents approve. If however, the experiment is done with the intention of later killing this living human to find out the results of the experiment, then a serious crime is committed against all human rights and we are back to the ethic for which certain Nazi doctors were executed after the trials of Neurenburg.

Experimentation can be done on living human tissue after the human dies. The death can occur either intra or extra uterine. Experimentation with or examination of dead bodies is ethical. Written consent from the patient, parents or next of kin is, of course, needed.

Remember, while in the uterus, this living human is technically called "fetus", after exit from the womb a "baby." The "pre-viable" fetus or baby is just as normal, healthy and alive as a "viable" one but is too small to survive unless he or she remains in the protective environment of the uterus.

Would you regard experiments on live human fetal tissue as ethical?

This is an entirely different question. When we die some types of our tissues can be preserved and classified as "live tissue." Experiments using live human tissue are entirely different from experiments on live humans.

Has there been any fetal experimentation in North America?

— Dr. A. Ammann of the University of California transplanted human fetal thymus glands into two older children. Both donor humans were killed.

Time Magazine, Feb. 28, 1972, p. 54

— Kidneys from aborted babies are being used to study kidney maldevelopment at Dalhouse University, Halifax, Nova Scotia, the donor humans are killed.

British Medical News, April 2, 1973

— Dr. R. Goodlin at Stanford University, California, did experiments including *"slicing open the rib cage of a still-living human fetus [newborn baby] in order to observe the heart action...some as old as twenty-four weeks....were used."*

Sworn testimony to Mary Swedsen
June 1, 1972

— *"It was repulsive to watch live fetuses [premature infants] being packed in ice while still moving and trying to breathe, then being rushed to a laboratory."* Seeing this happening at Magee-Womans Hospital, in Pittsburgh, she requested to be excused from helping with abortion. Her request *"was denied...with threats of being fired, harassment, intimidation, restrictions in assigned duties, etc."* She finally quit her job.

Testimony, Mrs. W. Pick, anaesthetist,
Pennsylvania Abortion Commission,
The Pittsburgh Catholic, March 17, 1972

— Researchers on the staff of the Colorado University Medical Center in Denver have used over 114 premature babies in experimentation on the lower jaw. The aborted babies had all been killed prior to the experimental procedures.

Am. J. Anatomy, Vol. 131, 1971

— Drs. Laphom and Marksbery report that they took human fetus brains and kept them alive as long as five months in explants. The donors were killed.

Science, Aug. 65

How about in other countries?

— Fig XII shows a baby being experimented on in a tank at Cambridge University, England.

— The most grisly one reported to date, was done at the University of Helsinki, Finland by Dr. Peter Adam, a professor at Case, Western Reserve University in Cleveland. In this experiment, babies, 12 to 20 weeks of age, were delivered alive and normal by hysterotomy (Cesarian Section). Their heads were then cut off and attached to a machine which pumped various chemicals through the brain circulation of their severed heads.

Medical World News, June 8, 1973, p. 21

— A six month aborted baby had his testicles transplanted into a 28 year-old Lebanese man who had been unable to become fully sexually active. The surgery was successful, the donor baby was killed.

Reuters News Agency, June 12, 1972

— The live beating hearts of preborn babies (up to 15 weeks) were removed for experimentation at the University of Szeged, Hungary.

Comparison of Spontaneous Contraction rates of in-situ and isolated fetal hearts in early pregnancy Resch. et al, Am. J. OB-GYN, Vol. 118, No. 1, Jan. 1, 1974

Is this still true?

In most countries yes, but the U.S. House of Representatives in April 1974 voted 281 to 58 to prohibit research on a human fetus "which has been removed from the womb and which has a beating heart." The Senate voted likewise adding only that the ban be reviewed later. A special commission later recommended that the total ban be lifted but suggested a number of restrictions.

The U.S. Congress also denied the U.S. National Science Foundation any funds "to be used to conduct or support research in the U.S. or abroad on a human fetus which has been removed from the womb, and which has a beating heart, unless such research is for the purpose of insuring the survival of that fetus [baby]."

What do most doctors think of live Fetal Experimentation?

It cannot be stated strongly enough that the overwhelming majority view this sort of activity as revolting, subhuman, barbaric, and disgusting and would categorically condemn it. When however, the door to abortion-on-demand is opened, things like this are bound to happen. Once reverence for life is lost at any stage of human life, practices like this soon appear.

Human Experimentation

THE LAST HOURS OF AN ABORTED BABY. Dr. Lawrence Lawn, of Cambridge University's Department of Experimental Medicine at work experimenting on a living, legally aborted, human baby. Some British doctors have been vigorously defending their experiments on live aborted babies after a storm of protest blew up in England when a Member of Parliament told the press that private abortion clinics had been selling live aborted babies for research. Dr. Lawn was quoted in the Cambridge Evening News as saying, "We are simply using something which is destined for the incinerator to benefit mankind .... Of course we would not dream of experimenting with a viable child. We would

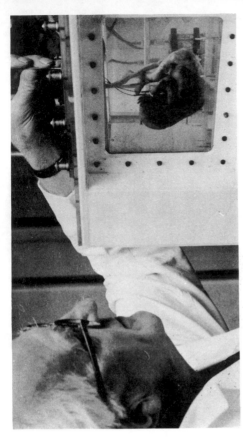

not consider that to be right". The Langham Street (abortion) Clinic, admitted sending aborted fetuses to the Middlesex Hospital which said that the fetuses 'were aged between eighteen and twenty-two weeks ... (The People, May 17, 1970). A spokesman for the clinic said that the fetuses 'were aged between eighteen and twenty-two weeks ... Our doctor had to give some special attention to the operation. He did this at his own expense and dispatched the fetuses to his colleague at the Middlesex Hopsital. It had to be done pretty promptly, but the hospital is only a couple of minutes away.' In the News of the World, for the same date, this same man, Mr. Philip Stanley, is also quoted as saying, "The position is quite clear. A fetus has to be 28 weeks to become legally viable. Earlier than that it is so much garbage".

Fig. XII (with permission, Minnesota Citizens Concerned for Life)

131

17

DOCTORS

I will give no deadly medicine to anyone if asked, nor suggest such counsel, and in like manner, I will not give to a woman a pessary to produce abortion.

The Oath of Hippocrates

I will not give my patients any poisonous drug, if they ask first, nor will I advise them thus, nor aid in a miscarriage.

Oath of the Arabian Physician

Hippocrates, the father of medical ethics, defined the practicioner of medicine as only a healer and thus began a new era. Previous to this, the medicine man's role had combined both that of healing and of killing. Today, turning the clock back several millenia, some doctors are again assuming that dual role. Just as the medicine man never had the complete trust of his patient then, today many wonder if they can now trust their obstetrician. Tomorrow it may also be their pediatrician and the rest of medicine.

On July 18, 1974 at the Annual Conference of the British Medical Association, the following motion was passed without dissent: "That this Meeting recommends that the British Medical Association adopt a policy that all medical schools throughout the country should consider introducing at their degree ceremonies the Declaration of Geneva 1948 which reads as follows:

> *"I solemnly pledge myself to consecrate my life to the service of humanity. I will give to my teachers the respect and gratitude which is their due; I will practice my profession with conscience and dignity; the health of my patient will be my first consideration; I will respect the secrets which are confided in me; I will maintain by all means in my power the honour and noble traditions of the medical profession; my colleagues will be my brothers; I will not permit considerations of religion, nationality, race, party politics, or social standing to intervene between my duty and my patient; I will maintain the utmost respect for human life, from the time of conception; even under threat, I will not use my medical knowledge contrary to the laws of humanity. I make these promises solemnly, freely, and upon my honour."*

The World Medical Association
Sept., 1948 Declaration of Geneva

Why was this "modern Hippocratic Oath" put forward as a motion to the British Medical Association?

It was put forward by doctors seriously concerned about the situation under the present British abortion law, and by the possible threat of legalized euthanasia. The fact that it was passed without dissent shows the support it was given.

Where does the A.M.A. stand?

There is a deep disagreement between members of the A.M.A. on the question of abortion. All that has been voted on approvingly by that House of Delegates is a rather carefully worded document which, in so many words, says that a doctor may do what the law says is legal.

Does making something legal, also make it right?

*In 1944, a physician in Germany could partici-
pate in genocide with legal sanction; In America he
would have been a murderer. In 1977, in America, a
physician can perform an abortion with legal sanction; in Germany, he would be a murderer. We have
come 360 degrees on the moral compass.*

Questions of Authenticity and Situational Ethics
M. Baten, W. Enos, Cancer Bulletin Vol. 29,
No. 4, 1978

Are there other medical organizations?

Yes, there are several. One that has spoken said
this:

*"Be it resolved that the Assembly and
House of Delegates of the Association of
American Physicians and Surgeons, Inc., in
regular session assembled in Chicago, Illinois
this 17th day of April 1971, deplores, con-
demns, and opposes so-called liberalization of
the indications for abortion by legislative action, treaty, executive order, judicial fiat, or
resolutions of medical or lay organizations or
societies."*

What do medical schools teach?

Since the discovery of conception over 100 years
ago and until about 10 years ago, it was taught that
human life began at conception, should be protected,
and that the only abortion that was ethical was a
"therapeutic abortion" to save the mother's life.

For the last decade, largely convinced that
"woman must have this right" most medical schools
have been justifying abortion on the grounds that
"the fetus is not yet human."

What of medical journals?

There has been a continuing flow of socially oriented articles on woman's rights, plus many on how to do the killing without hurting the mother.

In the past five years, your authors have seen very few articles, for general physicians, well illustrated, that inform doctors of the new and startling advances in Fetology, that confirm, if such is needed, the full humanity of the unborn.

You mean, doctors are not informed?

That is true. This is not necessarily a criticism of doctors who commonly are narrowly specialized. A brain surgeon doesn't know much fetology. A surgeon or an internist doesn't know much fetology. Unless the doctor actually treats or delivers babies or has studied the area he or she may know only what is remembered from medical school plus recent knowledge from Time Magazine, the Journal articles (above) and similar biased input from an occasional medical meeting, etc.

It is, incidentally, the rare doctor who has actually done or witnessed an abortion, especially a late one. We have commonly appalled most doctors in our audience when we have shown the short "suction abortion" movie (a clinical teaching film available from Cincinnati Right to Life.)

Those doctors closest to the problem, Neonatologists, are almost all firmly opposed to abortion. The specialty most in favor, Psychiatry, is the group furthest removed from obstetric and pediatric care.

What of other countries like England?

The Consultants of the Royal College of Obstetrics and Gynecology were polled in depth as to their opinions about abortion. The results were most interesting.

Do you favor abortion-on-demand?"

No	— 92%
Yes	— 4%
No answer	— 4%

Eighty percent felt that, if abortions were performed, that they should be done only by a consultant gynecologist and in a hospital, but only 21% of the doctors were willing to actually do any of the abortions themselves.

Of the physicians doing abortions, 75% had encountered opposition, from their nursing staffs, to their performing abortions. (It is interesting that Britain is less than 10% Catholic.)

Two-thirds of the gynecologists felt that the fact of their performing abortions would cut down on the number of young physicians interested in entering their specialty.

British Med. J. May '70

Only 4% of British gynecologists now favor abortion-on-demand?

Yes. This was a point of great annoyance to the Royal College, which spoke of it several times, speciafically: *"When the abortion bill was under discussion, its advocates repeatedly assured the Houses of Parliament that abortion-on-demand was not their object. Had they done otherwise, it is unlikely that the bill would have become law. Once the bill was passed, however, there has been a persistent and intense campaign which has had the effect of making the public believe that any woman has a right to have a pregnancy terminated if she so wishes."*

What is the motivation of the minority of doctors who are in favor of abortion-on-demand?

Unquestionably, some of the physicians who favor this view are sincere people who do it for idealistic reasons.

Unquestionably also, a fair percentage of those who are pushing hard for this are going to financially exploit it to the limit.

You mean doctors would do these just to make money?

There are a small number who abuse this in the most blatant fashion. Where vast sums of money are involved, the temptation for some is too great. A physician, describing his experience in doing abortions in New York said: *"Financially, after years of struggling, I can't help feeling a little like the Texan who drilled for water and struck oil."*

"SUDDENLY I'M A LEGAL ABORTIONIST"
Medical Economics, November 23, 1970

In a subsequent issue a prominent obstetrician relates how he was approached to lend his name and prestige to a small private hospital set up specifically to perform abortions: *"A syndicate invited me to be its medical director for up to $250,000 a year."*

"THE WILD SCRAMBLE FOR ABORTION MONEY"
Medical Economics, Jan. 4, 1971

One clinic of 5 physicians, working only in the mornings, at the cut-rate fee of $140.00 (cash) per abortion, has been "doing" 28 daily. From this part of their practice each is making $200,000/year.

The following ad was run in the Dallas Morning News 6-24-74. Guess why they were willing to pay over four times the starting salary for regular obstetric practice.

In what other ways is money made from abortions?

In a New York State Health Committee hearing in March, 1971, Senator Tarky Lombardi from Syracuse described a New York City abortion referral agency which, since July, 1970, had already paid a $64,000 dividend on a $1,000 investment.

A.M.A. News, March 15, 1970

Are doctors ever forced to do abortions against their conscience?

Pressure is exerted in many ways, few of them direct,

— A Gynecologist wants to join a partnership but will not be asked unless he'll do abortions.

— A pre-med student is interviewed for admission to a medical school, he is asked if he will do abortions.

— The same is true for admission to some nursing schools.

— A doctor in a teaching post will not get promoted unless?

— A surgeon who refuses to abort another doctor's patient may not get any more referrals.

How about overseas?

In England and other countries with socialized medicine a Gynecologist must get a government appointment. Because of this pro-life doctors are leaving these countries.

"I have personal knowledge of at least six cases in which highly trained and well-qualified doctors have been forced to leave the United Kingdom because they are Catholics."

The Tablet, February 5, 1972, p. 198

What of Germany?

Delegates of the German Medical Association voted 98% against abortion-on-demand. When asked why such an overwhelming majority voted against abortion, your authors were told *"because we've been through this once before and we know what it will lead to."* (euthanasia).

Seigfreid Ernst, M.D.
Town Councilman, Ulm
Member Luthern Synod

How about France?

In June of 1973 after the government had proposed legalizing abortion Professor Jerome LeJuene dramatically presented to that nation the signatures of over 10,000 physicians calling for full protection of human life by law from conception. This effectively stopped the law. By the spring of 1974 the number had grown to over 17,000 out of a total of 50,000 practicing physicians. Pro-abortionists were able to get only 300 signatures, almost 100 of which were shown later to be invalid.

In Belgium and Holland almost one third of practicing doctors have also signed the same statements.

18

RELIGION, VALUES, HISTORY

Abortion was known and commonly practiced in the world of Greece and Rome into which Christianity came. Judaism, having developed a high respect for the family, for women, and for individual life, had condemned abortion but found certain exceptions to it. The Christian message brought a further dignity to the concept of the individual person and the value of his life. The idea of an individual, animate immortal soul given by God to every human person and hopefully returning to him for eternity, was a powerful concept which, within two centuries, transformed the Roman Empire. The value of the born person became associated closely with a similar value granted to the unborn person, and as Christian beliefs crystallized in writing and tradition, condemnation of abortion came to be *"An almost absolute value,"* as Professor John T. Noonan of the University of California says in his book.

THE MORALITY OF ABORTION,
Harvard University Press, 1970.

The Gospel taught specifically that Jesus was conceived in Mary's womb by the Holy Spirit. What grew in her womb from conception was not a blob of protoplasm but the person of the God-man Jesus. Also clearly taught was that the infant John (the Baptist) *"leaped"* in the womb of Elizabeth. These specific references to the living personhood of the embryo were reinforced by the teachings of the Fathers of the Church. The Didache said, *"You shall not slay the child by abortions."* Clement of Alexandria condemned abortion, as did Athenagoras: *"Those who use abortifacients are homicides."* Tertullian said, *"The mold in the womb may not be destroyed."* The Council of Ancyra in 314 denounced women who *"slay what is generated."* Another Council in 305 at Alvira excommunicated women committing abortion after adultery and would not even re-admit them to the Church at the point of death. While Sts. Jerome and Augustine questioned when the rational soul was given by God, this did not affect their complete moral condemnation of abortion. In the late fourth century, St. Basil wrote, *"The hair-splitting difference between formed and unformed makes no difference to us. Whoever deliberately commits abortion is subject to the penalty for homicide."*

The early Christians saw their attitudes to women, children and the structure of the family as distinctive and revolutionary. The second century Epistle to Dionysius proclaims that Christians *"live in their own countries, but only as sojourners. They have a share in everything as citizens, and endure everything as aliens. Every foreign land is their fatherland, and yet for them every fatherland is a foreign land. They marry, like everyone else, and they beget children, but they do not cast out their offspring."*

By the time the curtain of the barbarian invasions rang down on the glory of Rome, the Christian teaching had codified itself into an extremely firm and certain moral opinion. Abortion was condemned. There was no question about Christian belief.

What was Thomas Aquinas's opinion 700 years later?

Thomas totally condemned abortion for any and all reasons. Interpretation of some of his thinking, however, has led some to assume that, if saving the life of the mother were the prime motive and action, and killing the baby a secondary effect, that this might have been permitted by Aquinas. This life-for-a-life ethic has been embodied in most state and national laws for over one-and-a-half centuries.

Aquinas did question when the soul was created. He spoke of the then-current scientific conviction that a male child was not fully enough developed to be judged human (and therefore to have a soul) until forty days, and that the female fetus could not be judged fully human until eighty days. This obviously says something about scientific knowledge of that age. Aquinas was reflecting a theological and scientific judgment that mirrored the most accurate scientific information of this time. When, to the most exact instrument available, the human eye, the unborn child looked like a child, it was deemed dignified and developed enough to be the possessor of an immortal soul, and so he made his conclusions.

The judgment of sexual differences echoed Aristotle's earlier thinking, and was a judgment based on when their eyes could identify in turn the penis (at 40 days) and the uterus (at 80 days).

Since that time, we have progressed to electron microscopes, ultrasonic stethescopes, an increasingly sophisticated knowledge of chromosomes and genes. We now must make judgments in the light of our new and more accurate biological knowledge. Aquinas's conclusions were the best that could be expected in his day. While not applicable today they are of historical interest. Had men of his time had today's knowledge of embryonic and fetal development, their conclusions would have been different.

When did some changes in the earlier absolute Christian position begin to occur?

In the centuries before and after the Protestant

Reformation, Christian thinkers came to debate and in some cases to justify the use of therapeutic abortion for the purpose of saving the life of the mother. Later, other reasons were added, such as the removal of an ectopic pregnancy (tubal pregnancy), or of a cancerous pregnant womb. Both of these killed the growing unborn child, if still alive, but were not direct assaults upon the child's life for the primary purpose of destroying it. Rather, they had another more primary effect of saving the mother's life. No major religious bodies came to endorse abortion for less serious reasons until the middle of the twentieth century.

What do Orthodox Jews believe?

The official Orthodox Jewish position is an almost total condemnation of abortion. The Rabbinical Council of America, representing 900 rabbis in the U.S. and Canada in a statement adopted unanimously by its 80 member policy making executive board called for the complete repeal of the permissive New York law and said that " . . . *the murder of these fetuses is a reflection of the hardening of human sensitivities characteristic of our age."*

"No woman is the final arbiter about the disposition of her body and the embryonic human life flourishing therein."

Abortion Law Scored by Rabbis
New York Times, April 24, 1972

In 1971 more than 700 Rabbis, assembled in Jerusalem, unanimously condemned abortion. Their spokesman Rabbi Jacob Kassen said:

"As Jews, who in our own lifetimes witnessed the most technologically and scientifically advanced nation in Europe methodically kill one third of our people — including the gassing and incineration of one million defenseless, officially unwanted Jewish babies — we have the most profound rea-

143

son to feel endangered, when, in the name of the so called advanced utilitarian 'new morality,' we see our own state (New York) begin to tamper with the sanctity of all human life."

Letter to New York State Legislators, May 16, 1971

And other Jews?

It is one of the strangest paradoxes of our time, in spite of this deep seated tradition, that most Jewish people in America not only favor abortion but number among their small percentage of the population a significant percentage of the leaders of the pro-abortion movement.

A major poll confirming previous similar ones, revealed that permission for abortion on social grounds alone (exceptions were the mother's life, serious health, rape, deformity) were

Catholics .... 23 - 34%
Protestants .... 27 - 55%
Jews .... 72 - 90%

Poll, DeVries and Associates, March 7, 1975

What is the Catholic position today?

The most authoritative statement in modern times was made by the Second Vatican Council, which specifically said, *"Life from its conception is to be guarded with the greatest care. Abortion and infanticide are horrible crimes."* This flat condemnation on abortion was directed to *"All men of good will."*

Isn't it true that Roman Catholic Church's complete condemnation of abortion dates only from 1869?

Absolutely not! The only aspect that has been subject to debate in the Catholic Church has been the time of ensoulment. Abortion, whether a soul has been judged present or not, has always been flatly condemned.

Aren't most people who oppose abortion Catholics?

Definitely not. Only 12% of the people of North Dakota are Catholic but 78% voted against an abortion-on-demand referendum.

The Utah legislature (1% Catholic) voted 66-1 against abortion. Kentucky (less than 10% Catholic) voted 34-4 in the Senate and 81-12 in the House, against abortion. Michigan (25% Catholic) voted 63% against abortion in their referendum.

One of the reasons that many people feel that most opposition to abortion is from Catholics is that almost one-fourth of the people of the U.S.A. are Catholic, many of whom do oppose abortion, and their opposition looms large. If, for example, one-fourth of the nation were Orthodox Jews, or were Mormons, they probably would be thought of as the main force against abortion.

What of the Mormon Church?

Joseph Smith, President of the Mormon Church, said, *"The destruction of life, even thought of as a fetus, is contrary to the whole concept of Christian living."*

What of Baptists?

By overwhelming vote 13½ million Southern Baptists resolved:
—that they reaffirm the view of the scriptures of the sacredness and dignity of all human life born and unborn
—opposition be expressed to all policies that allow abortion-on-demand
—that we abhor the use of tax money for tax supported non-therapeutic abortion
—that we favor appropriate legislation and/or a Constitutional amendment prohibiting abortion except to save the life of the mother

Southern Baptist Conv. June 1980, St. Louis

Did both Luther and Calvin condemn abortion?

Yes, John Calvin wrote "the unborn, though enclosed in the womb of his mother, is already a human being, and it is a most monstrous crime to rob it of life which it has not yet begun to enjoy. If it seems more horrible to kill a man in his own house than in a field, because a man's house is his most secure place of refuge, it ought surely to be deemed more atrocious to destroy the unborn in the womb before it has to come to light."

John Calvin, Commentary, Exodus 21:22.

What about the Church in Scotland?

"Though poles apart of vital doctrine from the Church of Rome we may yet join with them in this Biblical regard for human life, including that of the unborn babe. Life of man made originally in the image of God is sacrosanct."

The Monthly Record,
Free Church of Scotland, May, 1974

Have an eminent Protestant theologians condemned abortion in modern times?

Four great Theologians come to mind. Karl Barth (Swiss Reformed Church) said, *"He who destroys germinating life kills a man."*

CHURCH DOGMATICS, T and T Clark, 1961, page 416

Deitrich Bonhoffer (Reformed Church) said, *"To raise the question whether we are here concerned already with a human being or not is merely to confuse the issue. The simple fact is that God certainly intended to create a human being and that this nascent human being has been deliberately deprived of his life and that is nothing but murder."*

ETHICS, McMillan, New York, 1955, page 130

Professor Otto Piper of Princeton (united Presbyterian Church) has stated that, *"We have no right to destroy new life."*

Professor Helmut Thielicke, (Lutheran) Professor of Religion at the University of Hamburg, specifically states, *"Once impregnation has taken place, it is no longer a question of whether the persons concerned have the responsibility for a possible parenthood. They have become parents."*

THE ETHICS OF SEX, Harper & Row, New York, 1964

What of the other great world religions?

Islam, Buddhism, and Hinduism, are all unequivocal in their opposition to abortion.

What right has any religious body to impose its morality upon a woman?

If this were a sectarian religious belief, there would be justice to such a complaint. In fact, this is not a religious question except in the broad sense of equal rights, dignity and justice for all.

If any religious group has imposed their belief upon a nation, it is the Secular Humanists. The U.S. Supreme Court has defined Humanism as a religion. The officer corps of the Pro-Abortion Movement is almost entirely made up of Humanists who have imposed their beliefs upon our nations.

This is a civil rights issue. It is a question of whether an entire class of living humans shall be deprived of their basic right to life on the basis of age and place of residence.

Perhaps the question should be turned around?

What right does a mother have to impose her morality upon her unborn child . . . fatally?

19

THE POOR, WAR, CAPITAL PUNISHMENT

A constantly repeated reason to justify abortion-on-demand is that restrictive abortion laws discriminate against the poor. It is stated that those with money can, in one way or another, obtain abortions if they really want them and that the poor simply cannot.

Isn't it true that restrictive abortion laws are unfair to the poor?

It is probably true that it is easier for a rich person to break almost any law, than for a poor person to do so. Perhaps the poor cannot afford all the heroin they want. Rich people probably can. Does that mean we should make heroin available to everyone? Not everything that money can buy is necessarily good. The solution is not to repeal laws, but to enforce them fairly. Laws restricting abortion can be, and frequently have been, adequately enforced.

But it's still basically unfair, isn't it?

What is unfair is that poor people have not been given an adequate education and an adequate opportunity to better themselves. We will not eliminate poverty by killing poor people. The problem of the poor and the under-educated is their destitution and their lack of opportunity to achieve a better life, not the fact that they have children. Some who live in ivory towers seem unaware of this, but poor people themselves are very much aware of it, as evidenced by the fact that they as a group have cut their birth rate much less than middle and upper class socio-economic groups.

But don't too many children add to the burden of their poverty?

Poverty is more than just a shortage of this world's goods. Poverty is also the lack of spiritual and cultural resources, and often accompanying it is despair, apathy, and helplessness. Those who lack material things, and often find their chances for improvement of their lot in life rather bleak, sometimes find that much of their personal fulfillment is the joy they find in their children.

Do poor people tend not to accept abortion?

The majority certainly have not up until this time. Neither have poor or under-developed or under-educated areas of the world in any significant numbers accepted methods of birth control. It is the middle and upper classes who have accepted and used these methods.

What is the answer then for the poor?

The humane solution is to attempt to raise their standard of living and to help them achieve a more dignified existence. By raising a family's expectations in life, and the degree of education which they hope their children will achieve, people have universally been motivated to limit the number of children they have, in order to take adequate care of those children they have already borne. This seems to be the only way that will consistently motivate people to voluntarily limit their family size.

Are these white people, black people, Indians? Of whom do you speak?

We speak of them all, particularly however, non-white people throughout the world who suspect that the imposition of birth control and abortion on their culture is the white man's method of genocide.

Genocide? Who said this?

Mr. Wm. Darity, head of the Dept. of Public Health, Univ. of Mass., said:

"The study found parallel increasing evidence of strong opposition to family planning among blacks, including such moderate black civil rights organizations as the Southern Christian Leadership Conference.

"Considerably more black males under 30 agreed that family planning programs were designed to eliminate blacks." Also they were *"Overwhelmingly opposed to sterilization and abortion, 'even if you had all the children you wanted' "*.

STUDY OF A NEW ENGLAND COMMUNITY
Planned Parenthood Conf., Kansas City, April, 1971

That's only one report.

The first National Congress on Optimum Population and Environment, Chicago, June 1970 was a major meeting where black fears of genocide surfaced in a dramatic way. All of the major pro-abortion organizations, Zero Population, Planned Parenthood, Sierra Club etc. were there. Speakers included Senators Packwood, Humphrey, Nelson, Secretary Wirtz and others.

The November 1970 **Population Bulletin** contains a first hand report of the seminars, black-white divisions, the swelling black discontent during the meeting, and the formation of a separate black caucus. Finally on the last day two leaders of the black caucus Felton Anderson and Dr. Alyce Gullattee challenged *"the population movement's threat of geno-cide against the blacks"* and announced the blacks were quitting the Congress.

Are there other signs of this?

Try Michigan where:

A very popular black legislator in Detroit, Rosetta Ferguson, accused the pro-abortionists of *"Black Genocide"* before the November '72 referendum. The only two counties that voted pro abortion were the most intellectual county, Ann Arbor, and the wealthist county, Birmingham Hills in Northern Detroit. The Black vote was 80% against abortion.

Or Los Angeles where:

Mary Ann Knight, M.D., a public health physician, was fired for revealing publicly that Chicano welfare mothers were being told to get abortions or lose their welfare checks.

Or New York where:

— *"Non whites accounted for 46.7% of the abortions performed on city residents in the year ending July 1, 1972."* Health Services Administrator Gordon Chase said *"while accounting for only 29.8% of the live births."*

Sunday News, October 8, 1972

— Bellevue Hospital, New York, serving largely low socio-economic minority races, is doing 2.3 abortions for every live birth.

Douglas G.W., Complications of Saline
Induction of Abortion. Cook County Hospital
December 16, 1972

Do you really think there is a complete free choice for welfare women.?

What do you think of tax money being used for abortion?

We believe that this is certainly forcing the morality of the Secular Humanists upon the rest of us. The

151

U.S. Supreme Court ruled that it is legal to kill un-born babies. That does not mean that we, who are opposed to this, must also pay for the killing.

It is also legal for us to own a car. This does not mean that you are therefore required to pay for our car.

How about Abortion and Capital Punishment?

Capital punishment when carried out "justly".

a)   is punishment for a capital crime

b)   kills a guilty person

c)   after being so judged by due process of law

Abortion however

a)   is not a punishment

b)   kills an innocent person

c)   without due process of law

How can an anti-abortionist be for Capital Punishment?

Most pro-life leaders are against Capital Pun-ishment including ourselves. There are some how-ever, who use the above distinctions to accept it in certain cases.

Perhaps the question should rather be asked, *"Why are so many who oppose war and capital pun-ishment willing to approve the much more personal violence of killing unborn human lives in abortion"?*

Incidently, the U.S. Congress in reinstituting cap-ital punishment for certain high crimes, voted unani-mously to spare a pregnant woman's life until after delivery because the child was innocent of the crime of his mother. This is directly contradictory to the Su-preme Court which ruled that this "fetus" was not a person and had no rights prior to birth.

U.S. Senate Bill 1401, 93rd Congress, 1973-74

What is the difference between Abortion and War?

The concept of self defense is well established. If a life is taken in such a case and proven to be unavoidable, the defendant is not guilty of a crime. War, if ever justified, would have to be justified on the basis of self-defense. It is naked aggression.

Abortion certainly cannot be said to be done in self-defense, (except perhaps to save the mother's life??)

Is there really any difference between burning the skin off a baby with napalm (who you can't see die), and burning the skin off a baby by a salt injection (who you can't see die)?

War is waged by the state. Abortion is killing by a private citizen.

WHAT HAPPENS TO THOSE WHO KILL?

"What happens to a man who lets the blood of another man? This is the real question, the tragic question. The question of bloodletting is not, from the point of view of tragic vision, interesting at all. But the question of consequences, of phychic change, of the corruption of man's spirit, this is very nearly the only question worth asking". . . . .

"What happens in the heads of those who accede to bloodletting as a social method? What happens to the social managers, to the intellectuals, to the action-ists, to the students when men turn toward death as a way of life."

No Bars To Manhood, By Dan Berrigan, 1970

(Editors note: The above was written about war. We believe it applies equally well to abortion.)

"Acts of great evil come easily to human nature. All that man's malleable conscience demands is a he-roically articulated excuse combined with the com-radeship of other evil-doers. In other words, if the end is seen as both important and virtuous, then any means will often do. And the burden of solitary guilt need not be born if great numbers are also practicing the obscenity.

It is easier for a man to kill if those around him are killing, and it is easier for a man to kill if he has killed before. All fanatical tyrants have known this, from ancient oriental chieftans to Torquemada to Hi-tler to Mao. The moral instincts of humans are gener-ally fragile, and if they are not constantly renewed by vigorous use, they wear away until they crumble completely.

Edwin A Roberts, National Observer, Jan. 18, 1971

She had a number tattooed on her arm when I examined her. The origin of the tattoo was obvious and familiar — Buchenwald. I asked her if she would like to have it removed by plastic surgery, but she de-clined. She said she would wear it to her grave, for it was her diploma from the school of life. "Doctor, I don't know where you learned what life is, but I know where I learned it. I don't even step on cock-roaches now."

James J. Diamond, M.D., America, July 19, 1969

154

20

LAW CHANGE
HOW DID IT HAPPEN

In primitive times, there were many theories of how human life began and grew. Most scientists "knew" that the man planted the total new being in the fertile soil of his wife's body. From this has come the agrarian terms of "planting the seed, fertile, barren" etc.

When microscopes were developed, sperm was discovered (by Hamm in 1677). It was seen to be a tadpole-like object and not at all a "little man." Even so, the books of those years show drawings of little men curled up in the sperm's head for they "knew" he was there. This was called a "Homunculus."

As the power of microscopes increased, it slowly became evident that there must be another explanation of life's beginnings. Perhaps the woman contributed something of this new being? This idea was discussed, more was learned and finally in 1827, Karl Ernst von Boar, published the first accurate description of the process of conception. This was observed in a rabbit in 1843 by Martin Berry but not actually seen in a human until the 20th century.

By the 1850's, the scientific and medical world came to fully accept the fact that the man and the woman each contributed half of the new human being. This event was called conception or fertilization. It was at this time that members of the American Medical Association went to the state legislatures to testify and inform them of this newfound scientific fact.

English Common Law, while condemning all abortion, had levied only mild penalities for abortion before "quickening." This was because they "knew" that the baby was not yet alive before that time. After quickening, or when she "felt life", it was "known" that life was present and very severe punishments were given for late abortions. When "life came to the child", "the child came alive." When the mother "felt life" or "felt the baby kick", then that life was given the full protection of the law.

In 1859, the AMA protested that the quickening distinction allowed the fetus rights "for civil purposes" but as "to its life as yet denies all protection." They protested against this "unwarrantable destruction of human life" calling upon state legislatures to revise their abortion laws and requesting the state medical societies "in pressing the subject."

Roe v Wade, U.S. Supreme Court 1973

The AMA report by 1871 summed up abortion *"we had to deal with human life."*

As the state lawmakers were taught the new scientific fact that human life didn't begin at quickening but rather at conception, the laws were changed. One by one, each stated ruled that human life should be equally and fully protected by law, not from quickening but from its actual beginning at coneption. Pro-abortionists have incorrectly called these "archaic" laws when in fact, they reflect modern scientific knowledge. They have attempted to explain their passage as due to a desire to protect women from the then substantital danger of abortion. There were many other elective operations that were far more dangerous and no other operation was outlawed.

The laws were passed because our legislatures became aware that human life began at conception and they meant to protect life from its beginning. The explanation fabricated by the pro-abortionists is so obviously false that it does little for their credibility on other issues.

When did the laws again change?

— For over 100 years and until 1967, all states fully protected all human life from conception, then the first permissive law was passed in Colorado.

— By June 1970, when New York passed the first abortion on demand law (24 week limit), it was the sixteenth state to allow abortion. Most of the others had allowed abortion only for very restrictive reasons.

— After that only *one* more state legalized abortion (Florida) while 33 states debated the issue in their legislatures and all 33 states voted against permitting abortion for any reason except to save the mother's life.

— In April 1972, New York repealed their law but Governor Nelson Rockerfeller vetoed the repeal and the law remained in force.

What of the State Courts?

In the late 1960's and early 1970's, pro-abortionists challenged the constitutionality of laws forbidding abortion in most states. In about 1/3 of the decisions, such laws were declared unconstitutional and varying degrees of abortions were permitted. (Most were states that had already legalized abortion). Two thirds of the state courts however, declared existing laws to be constitutional.

Then there were referenda?

Yes, after the pro-abortionists were stopped in the

legislatures and in the courts, they tried referenda in two states. (abortion on demand until 20 weeks).

— North Dakota, only 12% Catholic, voted 78% against abortion.

— Michigan, an industrial state, voted 63% against abortion.

The tide had turned?

Yes, it seemed obvious that most people did not want abortion. But on January 22, 1973, the U.S. Supreme Court ruled.

Specifically what did the court rule?

The most fearsome holding of the U.S. Supreme Court was that a woman had a "right to privacy" broad enough to include abortion (her right to private killing). This was declared to be her basic constitutional right.

It also removed legal personhood from the unborn stating "legal personhood does not exist prenatally" thus removing the unborn's right to civil rights and equal protection by law.

What was the effect of the Ruling?

It struck down all laws against abortion in all 50 states.

— No legal restrictions at all upon abortion in the first three months.

— No restrictions from then until viability except those needed to make the procedure safe for the mother.

— Abortion was allowed until birth if one licensed physician judged that it was necessary for her "Health" (which they defined).

How did the U.S. Supreme Court define "health?"

The court said that abortion could be performed

"...in the light of all factors — physical, emotional, psychological, familial, and the

woman's age — relevant to the well being of the patient. All these factors may relate to health."

Doe vs Bolton, U.S. Supreme Court, No. 70-40, Page 11, January, 1973

"Maternity or additional offspring, may force upon the woman a distressful life and future. Psychological harm may be imminent. Mental and physical health may be taxed by child care. There is also the distress for all concerned associated with the unwanted child, and there is the problem of bringing a child into a family already unable, psychologically or otherwise, to care for it. In other cases the additional difficulties and continuing stigma of unwed motherhood may be involved. All these are factors that the woman and the responsible physician will consider in consultation."

Roe vs Wade, U.S. Supreme Court, No. 70-18, Page 38, January, 1973

But these reasons are social reasons, not health reasons?

That is the situation! The U.S. Supreme Court has specifically defined the word "health" to include a broad group of *social* problems, as judged by the mother herself. It has further specifically forbidden any state to forbid abortion at any time prior to birth for these reasons, if she can find a doctor to do the abortion. (all she needs is money).

Then the United States has abortion on demand until birth?

Correct, this is the legal situation.

How did the court justify its action?

It seems obvious that the court approached the issue with a clear conviction that "a woman must have this right" and tried to justify this right. They admitted that their decision was not in the Constitution but claimed that it was implied. They used almost every pro-abortion argument available including a number so false as to be almost ridiculous, and totally ignored a vastly larger body of firm scientific facts that would have completely refuted those arguments.

Specifically?

The most frightening is their insistance that even though they didn't know when "life" begins that they would rule out all protection for this growing living human being on the basis of age and place of residence.

They justified this civil rights violation because the fetus had not yet reached *"the capability of meaningful life"* that they are not *"persons in the whole sense."*

U.S. Supreme Court, ROE v WADE
IX, X

All of the euthanasis bills introduced so far justify post-born extermination when the patient is no longer capable of "meaningful" life.

What can states do to protect human life?

They can pass varying degrees of restrictive laws that discourage and regulate abortions but they cannot forbid it. Also 19 states have issued a call for a Constitutional Convention to send a Human Life Amendment to the States for ratification.

Can the U.S. Congress do anything at all?

Yes! Increasingly the U.S. Congress has been passing pro-life bills.

— To cut off federal funding for Medicaid abortions

- To stop abortions in military hospitals
- To stop pro-abortion legal action by government lawyers
- To limit fetal experimentation
- To stop overseas aid for abortions
- To aid pregnant women
- To take abortion out of family planning aid

The decision can only be reversed by an amendment to the U.S. Constitution?

Yes, unless the Court would reverse its decision which is unlikely.

How could such an amendment be passed?

It must first pass both houses of the U.S. Congress by a 2/3 vote. Then three-fourths of the state legislatures must ratify it by majority vote.

Has such an amendment been proposed?

Yes, after a full year of in-depth reevaluation, every one of the fifty state Right to Life groups agreed upon the amendment that they ultimately want. It is:

HUMAN LIFE AMENDMENT

Section 1: The right to life is the paramount and most fundamental right of a person.

Section 2: With respect to the right to life guaranteed to persons by the fifth and fourteenth articles of amendment to the Constitution, the word "person" applies to all human beings, irrespective of age, health, function, or condition of dependency, including their unborn offspring at every stage of their biological development including fertilization.

Section 3: No unborn person shall be deprived of life by any person: provided, however, that nothing in this article shall prohibit a law allowing justification to be shown for only those medical procedures required to prevent the death of either the pregnant woman or her unborn offspring as long as such law requires every reasonable effort be made to preserve the life of each.

Section 4: Congress and the several States shall have power to enforce this article by appropriate legislation.

How about an amendment that would allow each state to decide?

This would be completely unacceptable. Compare it again with Slavery. *The* problem was that each state could decide. That's why there was a civil war.

In matters of basic civil rights, the guarantee must be for all humans regardless of place of residence (womb) or of place of residence (a certain state).

21

TWO INFAMOUS DAYS
IN THE U.S.A.

On March 6, 1857 the U.S. Supreme Court finally decided a very vexing question that had troubled the citizens of the United States for many years. In the landmark Dred Scott decision they ruled once and for all that black people were not legal "persons" according to the U.S. Constitution. A slave was the property of the owner and could be bought and sold, used or even killed by the owner at the owner's discretion. The ruling was final, it was by the highest court in the land.

Or was it? Eleven years and a civil war later, in 1868 the people of the U.S. voted into effect the 13th & 14th Amendments to the U.S. Constitution. The interpretation of "person" was broad and included all living humans. It was crystal clear.

a) Life and its right to protection in law is not conferred by the state.

b) Legal personhood is not confered by virtue of color, age, or class.

c) Once human life exists, legal personhood exists.

On January 22, 1973 the U.S. Supreme Court finally decided a very vexing question that had troubled the citizens of the U.S. for many years. In a land-mark decision they ruled once and for all that unborn humans were not legal "persons" according to the U.S. Constitution. An unborn baby is the property of the owner (mother) and she can have the baby killed at her request, or because of her social distress ("health"). This can be done at any time until birth.

The ruling is final. It is by the highest court in the land.

Or is it? It could yet be overturned by a constitutional amendment. A new amendment could return to unborn people all the constiutional rights that born people have.

Then the discrimination was on the basis of skin color. Now it is on the basis of age and place of residence.

OTHER SUPREME COURT DECISIONS

— A husband has no right to protect the child he has fathered in his wife's womb. She can have it killed over his protest.

—A minor girl has the legal right to get an abortion without her parent's consent.

Danforth v Planned Parenthood, Bellotti v Baird, 1976

— Even though viable a child has no right to be delivered alive but can be killed by abortion if the abortionist wants to.

Colatti vs Franklin, 1979

— Federal, state and local governments have the complete right to use but also to not use tax money to pay for abortion

Harris vs McCrae, 1980

— Parents of a minor daughter have the right to be notified before she has an abortion.

H. L. vs Matheson, 1981

TODAY'S SLAVE . . . THE UNBORN CHILD

SLAVERY 1857	ABORTION 1973
Although he may have a heart and a brain, and he may be a human life biologically, a slave is not a legal person. The Dred Scott decision by the U.S. Supreme Court has made that clear.	*Although he may have a heart and a brain, and he may be a human life biologically an unborn baby is not a legal person. Our U.S. Supreme Court has just made this clear.*
A black person only becomes a legal person when he or she is set free. Before that time, we should not concern ourselves about him because he has no legal rights.	*A baby only becomes a legal person when he is born. Before that time, we should not concern ourselves about him because he has no legal rights.*
If you think that slavery is wrong, then nobody is forcing you to be a slave-owner. But don't impose your morality on somebody else!	*If you think abortion is wrong, then nobody is forcing you to have one. But don't impose your morality on somebody else!*
A man has a right to do what he wants with his own property.	*A woman has a right to do what she wants with her own body.*
Isn't slavery really something merciful? After all, every black man has a right to be protected. Isn't it better never to be set free than to be sent unprepared, and ill-equipped, into a cruel world? *(Spoken by someone already free)*	*Isn't abortion really something merciful? After all, every baby has a right to be wanted. Isn't it better never to be born than to be sent alone and unloved into a cruel world?* (Spoken by someone already born)

- The unborn baby is now the modern Dred Scott. As with a black slave then, the unborn baby now has no legal rights, is the "property" of the owner (mother), and can be killed if the owner wishes, any time before birth.
- The 14th Amendment to the Constitution was enacted specifically to overturn the Dred-Scott decision.
- Nothing but another Constitutional Amendment can overturn this recent dreadful decision.
- If you would respect all human life, black or white, born or unborn, young or aged, mother or baby, then . . .

**JOIN US! . . .
IN A MAJOR CONTINUING EDUCATIONAL EFFORT IN
SPEAKING FOR THESE TINY ONES WHO CANNOT SPEAK
FOR THEMSELVES**

22

LEGAL RIGHTS OF
THE CHILD

*"We hold these truths to be self-evident;
that all men are created equal, that they are
endowed by their Creator with certain unalienable rights, that among these rights are
life. . .*

*. . . that to secure these rights, governments
are instituted among men. . ."*

Declaration of Independence

*"Nor shall any state deprive any person
of life, liberty, or property without due process of law, nor deny to any person within its
jurisdiction that equal protection of the
laws."*

14th Amendment, Constitution of the U.S.

*"The child, by reason of his physical and
mental immaturity, needs special safeguards
and care, including appropriate legal protection, before as well as after birth."*

Declaration of the Rights of a Child
General Assembly of the United Nations
November 20, 1959

Almost without exception, every state, came to
put a law on its books granting equal protection of
the law of all humans regardless of age, place of

residence or degree of perfection. Worded in different ways, sometimes in even vague or unscientific terms, the meaning of these laws remained entirely clear to every one until the present decade. They simply meant that abortion was a crime and was forbidden by the laws of the state unless it was necessary to preserve the life of the mother. No other indications were recognized, except a variance of the above which spoke of serious threat to her physical health or life.

The major paradox within the legal community in modern times has been the rapid acceptance of the rights of the unborn child to all sorts of legal protection, safeguards, and redress from harm. In the fact of this had come an increasing permissiveness by some courts and legislatures to deny the unborn child the most basic right of all, the right to life. Then the U.S. Supreme Court ruling suddenly swept away all protection for unborn humans.

How long has an unborn child had the right of inheritance?

As early as 1795, the court interpreted the ordinary meaning of the word "children" in a will to include a child in the womb. The court: *"An infant (in the womb) who by the course and order of nature is then living, comes clearly within the description of 'children living' at the time of the decease (of the person who makes the will)."*

Doe v. Clarke 2H. Bl. 399, 126 Eng. Rep. 617

Further, in 1798, the court said that unborn children are *"entitled to all the privileges of other persons."*

Thelluson v. Woodford 4 Ves. 277, 31 Eng. Rep. 117

Several other decisions might be mentioned, including one in 1927 where a trust fund originating from the estate of the deceased was to be divided into *"as many parts as I have grandchildren living at the date of my decease"*. The person willing the property died on May 22, 1922. A granddaughter of the deceased was conceived on May 1, 1922. The court ruled that the granddaughter was entitled to a share in the estate.

Swain v. Bowers, 91, Ind. 307, N.E. 598, 1927

But didn't Justice Oliver Wendell Holmes in 1884 rule that an unborn baby was "not a person" in the eyes of the law? (Deitrich v. Northhampton).

This is true but Professor William Prosser, states that the reversal of the Deitrich doctrine *"has been sweeping."* Practically every jurisdiction that has considered the issue in the last generation has upheld the right of an infant to sue for injuries prior to birth.

Law of Torts, 3rd Edition

Can a child sue for injuries prior to birth?

This also, as Professor W. Prosser above has written, has become a completely accepted practice in our time. Children injured in the Thalidomide tragedy, some of them from pills taken as early as two to three weeks after conception, have consistently won court decisions granting them sums of money for their support because of the deformities they suffered from the drug while in the uterus.

Injuries received by an unborn child in his/her mother's womb from auto accidents have been fairly common and recoveries have been consistently granted.

But these were only granted to the children after they were born, not while yet unborn.

True to an extent. At first, awards were limited to those cases in which the child was born alive, and either died from injuries or remained alive with some handicap. More significant, however, has been a more recent trend allowing the parents or survivors to institute such an action even when the child is stillborn.

168

Therefore, an unborn child, who dies within the womb as a result of an accident, and who never experiences life outside of the womb has still been held to be "a person" who can sue for damages because of his death.

Louisell, "Abortion, the Practice of Medicine and the Due Process of Law," 16, UCLA Law Rev. 233, 1969.

Give an example.

The Massachusetts Supreme Court in April of 1927 in allowing recovery of damages for the wrongful death following prenatal injury said: *"In the vast majority of cases where the present issue has arisen, recovery has been allowed . . . To the extent that the views of text writers and legal commentators have come to our attention, they are unanimously of the view that non-viability of a fetus should not bar recovery."*

It further held that the unborn child was a *"person"* in the eyes of the law.

TORRIGAN V. WATERTOWN NEWS CO., 352 Mass. 446, 225 N.E. 2nd 926, 1967

I've heard an unborn child can get social security benefits. Is this true?

A recent decision by the U.S. Court of Appeals for the Fifth Circuit (1969) verified this. The father of an illegitimate child was killed a short time after the child was conceived. The right of the child to receive social security benefits on the earning record of the father depended on whether the father was "living with" the child at the time he died. The court held that the unborn child was living with the father at that time, and said: *"Medically speaking, Donna was viable from the instant of conception onward. An action for damages would have been brought in her behalf for injuries she might have received prior to birth. When the deceased wage earner came over for his weekend visits, he was in fact living with both child and mother."*

Wagner v. Gardner, 413 F2d 267

What other rights does the unborn child have legally?

He can have a guardian appointed, can ask for an injunction, and may be an executor.

In 18 states, (since the Supreme Court Decision) authorities have decided that a pregnant woman can receive welfare payments for her unborn child, just as for any other child.

Time Magazine Oct. 1973

Have there been any cases of an unborn child suing even before his birth?

Recent advances in the medical science of fetology have made it possible to treat the "littlest patient" prior to birth. One such new advance is the possibility of giving a blood transfusion to a baby while yet in his mother's uterus who would otherwise die because of an Rh problem. In just such a case, the child's mother, a member of a religious sect forbidding blood transfusion, refused to allow an intra-uterine blood transfusion for her unborn child. She objected to the invasion of her own body, stated she had a right to "privacy", and also that this violated a firmly held religious conviction of hers. The New Jersey Supreme Court noted that her right to freely practice her religious belief was one of the most fundamental and sacred constitutional rights, and that her right to her own body was also a basic right. It clearly decided, however, that this right would have to be subordinated to the unborn child's right to survival, which it stated, was a value outweighing the parent's constitutional right to practice in this manner her religious beliefs.

Fitkin v. Anderson 42 N.J. 421, 201 A. 2d 537, 1964

Another such case involved a mother, four months pregnant who, following surgery, was dying from loss of blood. She refused a blood transfusion for herself on religious grounds. The court ordered her to have the transfusion saying that she had the religious right to refuse for herself but not for her unborn child.

Chicago Circuit Court, May 1971, Judge Albat Kvistadt

Before the 1973 decision, most state courts had upheld the right of the unborn to equal protection by law. Could you give examples.

"The phenomenon of birth is not the beginning of life, it is merely a change in the form of life." "A fetus having died in its mother's womb is dead. It will not come alive once separated from her. A fetus living within the womb is a living creature. It will not die when separated from her unless the time, the manner, or the circumstances constitute a fatal trauma" ... *"the fact of life is not to be denied, neither is the wisdom of the public policy which regards unborn persons as being entitled to the protection of the law."*

July 7, 1971, Michigan Supreme Court

"...unborn children have all the qualities and attributes of adult human persons differing only in age or maturity. Medically, human life is a continuum from conception to death."

"The [U.S. Supreme] Court generally expressed its disapproval of the practice of putting to death persons who, some would argue, had forfeited their right to life. We believe we must anticipate at least equal solicitude for the lives of innocents."

Missouri Supreme Court, October 1972,
ROGERS VS DANFORTH

"The legal conclusions in Griswold as to the rights of individuals to determine without governmental interference whether or not to enter into the process of procreation cannot

*be extended to cover those situations wherein,
voluntarily or involuntarily, the prelim-
inaries have ended and a new life has begun.
Once human life has commenced, the Constitutional protections found in the Fifth and
Fourteenth Amendments impose on the state
the duty of safeguarding it."*

STEINBERG V. RHOADES, C70-289, U.S. District Court,
Northern District of Ohio, Jan. 1971

Have there been many decisions supporting the rights of the unborn child before he is "viable"?

The Supreme Court of South Carolina specifically held that an action for wrongful death on behalf
of a stillborn child could be maintained in that state
and noted that "a slight majority" of American ju-
risdictions allow the maintenance of such a cause.

FOWLER V. WOODWARD, 148 S.E. 2d 142, 1964

Judge Haynsworth spoke forcefully to this matter: *"It seems to be evident that limiting recovery in
these cases to injuries suffered after the child becomes
viable is a social perversion without support in reason
or historical precedents. Viability of the child at the
time of injury ought to be recognized as the imposter
it is and sheared of all future influence upon our
judgments."*

341 F 2d at 79

In 1965, the Supreme Court of the United States recognized the right of marital privacy in voiding a law preventing the dissemination of contraceptive devices (Griswold v. Connecticut). The U.S. Supreme Court has now radically extended this "right of privacy" to allow abortion. What do you think?

The best answer to this was given when the Ohio
Abortion law was ruled constitutional

*"This court . . . believes that the cases that
do accept (this association) have not been*

*based on a proper legal factual under-
standing. The plaintiff's contentions seek to
extend far beyond the holdings in the
Griswold case this "right of privacy,' which is
nowhere expressly mentioned in the constitution or its amendments, but is found
only in the 'penumbra' of those articles.
Rights, the provision of which is only implied or deduced, must inevitably fall in con-
flict with the express provisions of the Fifth
and Fourteenth Amendments that no person
should be deprived of life without due process
of law. The difference between this case and
Griswold is clearly apparent for here there is
an embryo or fetus incapable of defending itself. There the only lives are those of the two
competent adults.*

*"Without going into all of the myriad of
cases and texts that deal with various aspects
of this problem, the question resolves itself
into whether the state has a legitimate interest
to legislate for the purpose of affording an
embryonic or fetal organism an opportunity
to survive. We think it has, and on balance it
is superior to the claimed right of a pregnant
woman, or anyone else to destroy the fetus except when necessary to preserve her own life."*

U.S. District Court, Northern District of Ohio,
STEINBERG VS RHOADES, Jan. 1971

What then is the chief legal objection to abortion?

a) The being in the womb is a living, total,
   growing human being by any scientific
   measurement.

b) Our legal system is founded upon the equal
   protection by law of all living humans

c) Discrimination by race, religion, origin, size,
   degree of perfection or dependency, place of
   residence, politics, etc., is a violation of the
   concept of equal justice.

d) This is a civil rights issue

e) The discrimination by abortion is on the basis of age and place of residence

The U.S. law now gives to one citizen (the mother) the absolute legal right to kill another (her unborn daughter)?

If this is done because:

— she is being burdened?

— she is being embarrassed?

— she is older, bigger and stronger?

— she is more conscious and smarter?

— she is poor?

— she can pay to have it done?

— the law allows it?

Then the inevitable logic of law will someday permit a daughter to have her mother killed because

— she is being burdened!

— she is being embarrassed!

— she is younger, bigger and stronger!

— she is more conscious and smarter!

— she is poor!

— she can pay to have it done!

— the law allows it!

Is this now, or will it be then, the private right of one citizen? Or isn't this the most public concern of all? Isn't it the duty of the state (all of us) to safeguard that one right without which no other right matters, the right to life?

ABORTION IN TODAY'S WORLD

— Marshal McLuhan's View —

In discussing the societal cause and effect of abortion, Marshall McLuhan stated that "Since all current secular discussion of abortion takes place on quantitative assumptions relating to human convenience, there can be no question that the arguments in favor of abortion, apply with equal validity to the status of all other living beings. The same assumptions of more or less convenience, or inconvenience, must apply to the decisions about continuing or suppressing the existence of any members or groups of all human or non-human populations."

Further, "When the mechanization of death occurs on a vast scale, the minds of civilized people are numbed. Decent and well meaning people, acting as if in corporate somnambulism, are engaged today in repeating in abortion centres the patterns of life processing which worked so well in meat packing and death camps. . . . One precedent begets another by echo of remorseless logic and quantified statistical reasoning. If meat packing and death camps can resonate in a way that makes abortion centres a familiar and acceptable pattern, the abortion centres themselves constitute a further precedent for the repetition of further violence to human dignity and compassion.

Further, "The outlook and the methods of the abortionists are borrowed from the preceding industrial age where significance was to be found in efficiency and in quantity. It is the decline of the human significance resulting from industrial goals and methods that now confronts both the exponents and the victims of abortion. Caught between the industrial quantitative values and the new life values of the electric age, many people are unable to perceive why they feel so unhappy about abortions while at the same time thinking that it is a plausible and enlightened program for the relief of man's congested estate."

Marshal McLuhan (author, THE MEDIA IS THE MESSAGE)
U. of Toronto, Centre for Culture and Technology
Personal Communication, August, 1972.

PART III

ACTION

23

CORRECT SOCIAL INJUSTICE

Space does not permit any major investigation or lengthy commentary here. Let this not, however, give any false impression. Correcting social injustice is, without question, the most important aspect of the entire abortion problem. Women want abortions because, in the vast majority of situations, they are in social or economic difficulties. To merely oppose abortion and do no more is not only useless, but frankly immoral. Anyone active in the pro-life movement should be equally as active in a wide variety of social actions.

*"Choosing abortion as a solution to social problems would seem to indicate that certain individuals and groups of individuals are attempting to maximize their own comforts by enforcing their own prejudices. As a result, pregnant school girls continue to be ostracized, mothers of handicapped children are left to fend for themselves, and the poor are neglected in their struggle to attain equal conditions of life. And the **only** solution offered these people is abortion. It becomes very disturbing when we think that this destructive medical technique may replace love as the shaper of our families and our society."*

*"We **must** move toward creating a society in which material pursuits are not the end of our lives; where no child is hungry or neglected; where even defective children are valuable because they call forth our power to love and serve without reward. Instead of destroying life, we should destroy the conditions which make life intolerable. Then, every child regardless of its capabilities or the circumstances of his birth, would be welcomed, loved, and cared for."*

INDUCED ABORTION, A DOCUMENTED REPORT, Preface,
Hilgers & Shearin,
Minn. Citizens Concerned for Life

Basic to the entire problem is the fragmentation of family life in this century. Anything that can be done to help restore the dignity and security of family life will go a long way toward eliminating the problems that seem to call for abortion. To restore the dignity of each man and woman in society is of utmost importance. To accept our human sexuality, joyfully, but also responsibly, is the job that is cut out for each of us. That we should work for racial justice should go without saying. Positive actions such as those in Chapter 25 and 26 should be implemented immediately. Responsible family planning is essential. So many other social wrongs cry for our attention, e.g. the billions being spent on bombs instead of people, the polluting of our planet, the outrage of our prisons, the abuse of some of our courts and legal processes rendering justice at times so difficult to come by — all of these and others are important. No one person can apply himself to them all. Our world needs each person's best efforts, with the responsibility resting heavily on those who have been given such a larger share of this world's gifts. Each can take different points of departure and try to make this world a little better place than the world each of us came into.

The problem of abortion, we believe, rates absolute top priority in the field of human problems that we have mentioned. It does so not simply because it is, in many ways, related to the problems above, but because, if permissive abortion becomes the practice of our countries, this fact itself will go a long way toward making many of the above problems worse. It would seem at first glance to some people that to kill off your problems eliminates the problems. In the long run, however, the philosophy of disrespect for human life that this entails erodes the very foundation stone of a stable society, and ultimately will cause far greater chaos and human misery than the somewhat easy solution it may present to some on the surface.

Both philosophies cannot coexist then?

"Even if a majority of citizens did favor legalization, and I think it does not, convictions so deep as those of the opponents of abortion must be taken into account if they are not to be wholly alienated from the body politic. The fact that no one who does not believe in abortion will be forced to engage in abortion (as yet) does not help. It is like telling someone in Nazi Germany 'Don't worry, your hands are clean, you don't have to guard the camps.' In order to go on supporting a government which he thinks kills the innocent, a person must surely begin to lose whatever moral standards he has. A nation of amoral beasts may be the result. Either that, or revolt. At least one New York Senator refused to agree to any aspect of a new budget as long as it contained money 'to kill babies.'"

Richard Stith, Commonweal, Nov. 12, 1971

What if abortion laws were reversed, what would be done with all the babies?

The answer is that if the mother can't or doesn't want to care for the child, it should be given to a couple who can.

How can a girl give up her own baby?

It takes maturity and love. It is completely normal to want to keep the baby. If however, she makes a judgment that she cannot give the baby the home, father, education, etc., that the baby needs, and if she thinks of the baby's needs ahead of her own, she may give the child to a couple who can, **because** she loves her baby so much.

"God so loved the world that He gave us his only Son"

"He so loved us that he gave us His life"

But think of the poor mother, going through life never knowing what is happening to the child she gave away?

Which is the better memory, to know that you gave your baby life, then because you loved him, gave him to the outstretched arms of a stable, loving husband and wife — or to remember that "I killed my baby."

Is there a shortage of babies to adopt?

Yes, in the U.S. in one year, there were 800,000 couples cleared and waiting to adopt but only 100,000 babies placed. Many maternity homes, have closed because so many mothers now kill their babies instead of delivering.

But what of the defective, biracial, older, and other hard to adopt children?

In areas where adoption agencies have publicized the availability of such children, with the exception of some older children almost all are now being placed.

Wouldn't there still be some left?

Perhaps yes. One partial answer is the passage of laws providing adoption subsidies. There are many families of very modest means who want children but cannot afford to adopt. Many of these are willing to accept and love these hard-to-place children. If a certain state allowance were provided, they could and would adopt.

Even the defective ones?

Yes, and this is one of the truly heartwarming recent developments. Here again, the state can help both. These parents and those who discover that their own baby, yet unborn, will be defective. A subsidy could be provided. What of the cost of special surgery? of special education? If parents knew that some help was available, they'd be more likely to a) adopt these children b) not kill their own before brith c) not put their own defective child in an institution.

Any other good ideas?

Yes. One major one. Today most insurance will pay for the cost of killing a baby by abortion whether the mother is married or not. However, few will give maternity benefits unless a) she is covered by a family contract and b) has been married over nine months.

This is rank discrimination against unmarried women. Some states have passed laws requiring all insurance carriers in that state to provide maternity benefits if a) she has had coverage for nine months and by a contract providing maternity benefits, (such as by her parents policy) but, b) she does not have to be married to collect.

24

FAMILY PLANNING

Among the positive alternatives that must be discussed, family planning ranks very high. Few today argue against responsible family planning. It has come to be an accepted value in our culture, endorsed as such by most concerned people and religious bodies. To say that a married couple should attempt to have only as many children as they can adequately care for is to respect a self-evident norm, a norm that most would agree with completely.

The right of a husband and wife to determine the number of children they wish is a right that should never be ursurped by the state. It is one of the most basic of all rights.

Unfortunately the term "Birth Control" which had included only natural and artificial methods of prevention of conception, now has been broadened by the anti-life people to also include abortion. Remember this when you allow your school to teach about "Birth Control."

What is the difference between Abortion & Contraception?

Contraception prevent human life from beginning. Abortion directly kills a human life already begun.

a) The legal freedom of individuals to use contraceptives has been recognized by most governments during this century. The recognition of such individual freedom of action does not, by itself, make such actions morally either right or wrong. Obviously, there are sharply differing judgements taught by different religions, e.g. the Roman Catholic Church forbids the use of artificial contraceptives on the grounds that human persons are no more the arbiters of the process by which human life comes to be than they are of human life already begun. If a husband and wife do decide to use contraceptive methods to plan their family, this decision immediately affects only themselves and their own bodily functions.

b) Abortion however, kills another human being. As such it can never be a matter of a mother's privacy or legal freedom of action (as ruled by the U.S. Supreme Court). Once pregnant, a woman is going to have a baby. The only choice open to her then is have her tiny son or daughter killed, or to allow the child to grow and be delivered. It should be the social concern of all citizens to give equal protection by law to all members of society.

This is a primary reason why *"Governments are instituted among men."* Do we give the mother the legal right to kill the two year old daughter who is a burden to her? No! Then why and how can we give her the legal right to kill the two month old daughter (who lives inside her) who is a burden to her?

What is an I.U.D.? (Intrauterine device)?

This is a small plastic or metal device that is inserted into the cavity of the uterus from below. The purpose of this is to "prevent" pregnancy.

Is an I.U.D. a contraceptive or an abortive agent?

With a few exceptions, almost all scientific papers agree that its effect is to prevent the implantation of the tiny new human being (blastocyst stage of development) in the nutrient lining of the uterus. This is clearly abortive.

Several papers have suggested a contraceptive action, such as destruction of the sperm by macrophage action (Acta. Cytol, Balt. 14:58-64, 1970); speeding the passage of the ovum through the tube so as to escape fertilization (T. Mastroianni, Med. World News, Nov. 6, 1974). Overwhelmingly, however, other papers, while referring to the process as "contraceptive" typically agree that

> "It is clear that an I.U.D. prevents pregnancy in women by interrupting the reproductive process prior to implantation of the [fertilized] ovum."

Davis, Lesinski, Mechansim of Action of Intrauterine Contraceptives in Women, Ob-Gyn Vol. 36, No. 3, Sept. 70.

The most comprehensive collection of scientific papers on this subject was prepared at the Mayo Clinic by Dr. Thomas Hilgers, currently at Creighton University, College of Medicine. It has been reprinted and made available by Dr. John Harrington, editor of Marriage and Family Newsletter.

The Intrauterine Device, Contraceptive or Abortificient? Marriage and Family Newsletter, Vol. 5, No. 1, 2, 3, 1974 P.O. Box 190, Midnapore, Alberta, Canada TOL 1J?

How about the "pill"?

There are over 30 "contraceptive" pills on the market, each differing a little from the others. They "prevent" pregnancy through three separate functions.

1) They thicken the mucous plug at the cervix. If this is the primary effect then it truly is contraceptive.

2) They prevent release of the ovum. If this is the primary effect then the function is sterilization.

3) They render the lining of the womb hostile to implantation. This effect is abortifacient.

In any one month for any one woman, which effect is primary? Who will ever know? Increasingly however, we know that the low dose pills, most widely used today, do allow ovulation and fertilization, at times, but act to destroy this tiny new human life by preventing implantation.

The "pill" does seem to be definitely abortive in action at times.

How does the "Morning After Pill" work?

It probably has an antinidatory effect on the endometrium, (i.e. a hardening of the lining of the uterus) which would preventing implanation of the tiny new human being (blastocyst stage). This effect is definitely abortive.

It almost certainly, at times, acts in a sterilizing fashion. The "massive" dose given rapidly effects the ovary, preventing a scheduled ovulation (and fertilization by the sperm present) that might have occurred 1-3 days after the intercourse.

Its use involves a small but real risk of blood clots to the woman (Canadian Health Dept.) and of later female cancer in a child born from a mother who took it (U.S. Food & Drug Administration).

What about sterilization?

From the viewpoint of family planning, surgical sterilization is a permanent form of preventing pregnancy. It can never be equated with abortion. It is a mutilation of a body system and a serious and irreversible one. It does prevent human life from beginning. It does not kill a life already begun.

While many would view this (sterilization) as totally unacceptable to them, the fact remains that, unlike abortion, sterilization does not take unborn human life.

What about compulsory sterilization for those who have major, dominant genetic defects which they would be passing on to their children?

Conscientious people with a hereditary defect would be well-advised to refrain from having their own children, but rather to adopt other children as their own if they desire a family. Compulsory sterilization for some such reasons has already been enacted into law in some states and nations. Not many would agree with this type of law and activity. Even this, however, is something essentially less than the deliberate taking of a human life once conceived, since this involves only that person's body and not the life of another human being as abortion does.

But family planning methods don't always work. What happens if a woman becomes pregnant and didn't want to be?

Over a lifetime, statistically speaking, most family planning methods do work. They also do fail in individual situations. Many people who are reading these words have been surprised by an unplanned pregnancy. Most of these originally unplanned pregnancies over a period of nine months, however, came to be wanted and after birth became very cherished and loved children indeed. Truly, family planning, while not always "working" in each individual instance will, if averaged out over a lifetime of marriage, in almost all cases be very effective indeed in producing a family of approximately the size that a particular couple would desire. In any case, one cannot solve such a "problem" by killing a baby.

What about Natural Family Planning?

This is not to be confused with the old (and relatively ineffective) calendar rhythm. Utilizing an intimate knowledge of the woman's bodily functions such as mucous production, body temperature, and other signs and symptoms, this method helps a couple know when her fertile and non-fertile times of the month are. Without using any pills or other artificial means, couples plan their families by having intercourse when she is not (or is) fertile.

What is Planned Parenthood's position on abortion?

In its early years of existence Planned Parenthood limited itself to contraception and specifically opposed abortion. The following is a quote from an official Planned Parenthood pamphlet.

"Is birth control an abortion?

Definitely not. An abortion kills the life of a baby after it has begun. It is dangerous to your life and health. It may make you sterile so that when you want a child you cannot have it. Birth control merely postpones the beginning of life."

Planned Parenthood, Aug. 1963

Today, Planned Parenthood is probably the most aggressive and powerful force in the world pushing for free abortion-on-demand for any woman, anywhere, for almost any reason at all. They are now dedicated to helping mothers find physicians who will *"kill the life of a baby after it has begun" (quoted above).*

25

THE BIRTHRIGHT CONCEPT

This ad appeared in the student newspaper of a major midwestern university.

ABORTION COUNSELING, INFORMATION AND REFERRAL SERVICES

Abortions up to 24 weeks of pregnancy are now legal in New York State. There are no residency restrictions at cooperating hospitals and clinics. Only the consent of the patient and the performing physician is required.

If you think you are pregnant, consult your doctor. Don't delay. Early abortions are simpler and safer.

If you need information or professional assistance, including immediate registration into available hospitals and clinics, telephone:

THE ABORTION  INC.

▨▨▨▨▨▨ STREET
NEW YORK, N. Y. ▨▨▨▨

The following week this "ad" appeared.

We are adoptive parents. Our children were given the gift of life by men and women other than ourselves. Our children live now because these women and men chose life instead of death. We can never comprehend the suffering they endured. But we shall always be thankful for their courage and generosity. Their gift of life shall flourish.

— A ▨▨▨▨▨▨ faculty member and wife

Which choice will the pregnant girl make? Death to the living one within her? Or will she give the child life?

Most mothers, if given help, will choose life. The problem is that society often gives her little alternative to abortion. For a variety of reasons, women have often not asked for help from existing agencies or have feared disclosure or red tape if they went to them. Now private groups have been formed to aid those who do not want abortions. What is needed is help for the distraught mother who isn't sure she wants an abortion.

In the face of this need, Birthright appeared.

What is Birthright?

Birthright, founded by Mrs. Louise Summerhill in Toronto, Canada, in October, 1968, has the creed: *"The right of every mother to give birth; the right of every child to be born."* She founded the first center which has been extremely successful. The idea has spread like a prairie fire through Canada and the United States to England, Europe and the rest of the world. Few pregnant women really want an abortion, but society, as mentioned, often forces them to make this choice. This service offers an alternative: encouragement to bear the baby, and help in finding the financial and medical assistance to do so. It operates centers for distressed pregnant women, offering a sympathetic ear, counselling, appropriate aid, guidance or referral to existing agencies or professionals for help.

Are there many of these groups and are they all called Birthright?

There are over 1,000 functioning centers in the U.S. alone and new ones are forming almost daily here and abroad.

The names vary; Lifeline, Heartbeat, Alternatives to Abortion, Birthright, Problem Pregnancy, Help, etc.

An international organization "Alternatives To Abortion" has been formed. This proposes to function as an umbrella, under and thru which all similar organizations could co-ordinate at least some of their activities while still remaining autonomous in their function or other affiliations.

The addresses are:

— Birthright, 699 Coxwell Ave., Toronto, Ontario

— Alternatives to Abortion, Suite 511, Hillcrest Hotel, Toledo, Ohio

How are they publicized?

Its number should be listed in the phone book, and frequently advertised in the daily papers so that it becomes a known service. For example, in Cincinnati, its number is Ah-1-LIFE (241-5433).

Does it work?

In the first three years of the Toronto service, Birthright assisted 2,500 girls. Of this large number, who were helped to have babies and to solve their personal problems, only 12 women are known to have repeated. Contrast this with one smallish Canadian hospital which in one year aborted two women three different times each. Note also California's record.

Contrast this with statistics from California.

In 1969, 55% of abortions were the first one for the woman. By 1972, only 38% of all abortions were the woman's first.

Second and third abortions have risen from 24% to 36%

Women having their 4th abortion now make up 22% of all abortions done.

Calif. Dept. of Health Report

What age women come for help?

Most have been single and between the ages of 16 and 25. However, women of all reproductive ages have been helped.

Are these organizations connected to any church?

These are private organizations. Most are completely non-sectarian, and independent. There are however, a few sponsored by churches. More power to them all.

Will a girl's parents be told, if she is a minor?

She is encouraged and offered help to do so, but her wishes in the matter will be respected.

Are records kept that could later reveal secrets?

No records are kept of any kind. She need not even give her right name. It is an entirely confidential service whose only purpose is to help the woman in distress.

What if the woman is without funds?

These groups will help her find the assistance she needs. This may include helping her find temporary employment, a home for her to live in, medical care, etc.

Is she advised to keep her baby or place it for adoption?

The decision is hers. Adoption help will be available if that is her choice.

What if she wants to keep the baby?

Approximately one-third of the girls helped have kept their babies. When this happens, the volunteer woman who has been helping the distressed pregnant woman will help her in any way needed, even obtaining baby clothes, crib, etc.

What if she needs counseling?

Medical, religious, economic or psychological help will be available if she needs it.

Who are the ladies who staff the phones?

They are all volunteers, usually married women, but not necessarily; well-balanced, stable, concerned ladies who want to help other women.

But what of the "Clergy Counseling Service" or similar groups? Don't they serve the same purpose?

Almost all "Clergy Counseling Service" groups and with few exceptions, also most Planned Parenthood agencies are truly abortion referral groups, they do not offer impartial counseling.

The question to ask about any group in your city is, "What percent of women who are counseled ultimately have abortions?" The Dayton (Ohio) Clergy Consultation Service on Abortion for instance, in 1971 referred 94.5% of its applicants for abortion. (Annual report of organization.)

Some of these groups work closely with abortion clinics and even receive financial reimbursement from them. One California "service" charges $350.00 of which:

> *"The doctor receives $75.00, the hospital $250.00, and Planned Parenthood $25.00."*

The Rev. Anwyl [director of Clergy Counseling Service, Planned Parenthood] *"admits that he is 'biased' in his counseling favoring abortion, because 'since religion has contributed to this mess we're in, I'm trying to counteract this.'"*

"Twelve thousand patients a year at $25.00 a throw amounts to $300,000.00 annually for Planned Parenthood Clergy Counseling. No mean income. Another such service, Problem Pregnancy Information Service, referred 20,000 women for abortions this year. That amounts to a half million dollars annual operation."

Abortion Tragedy in Hospital,
H. Koblin, Los Angeles Free Press,
September 15, 1972, Page 13

Why did Mrs. Louise Summerhill start this organization?

Let's let her speak for herself:

"The conditions that make a child unwanted must be changed. I question the credibility of anyone who is for or against abortion unless he is working to change conditions and attitudes.

"Allowing a woman to empty her womb, particularly a teenager, treats only the symptom, not the cause. The teenager may be striking out at her parents or looking desperately for affection. Psychologists say most women get pregnant deliberately, even though they may not realize it. Such a person is likely to be a repeater. We had one teenager whose mother had arranged for her to have two abortions. She was pregnant again, and came to Birthright because she wanted to have the baby.

"If a woman carries her baby to term, she is more likely to realize that she must take some responsibility for her sexuality, and that through sexual intercourse she may create another life."

193

26

RIGHT TO LIFE

Right to Life organizations have been and are being formed in many areas. Primarily educational groups, their urgent goal is to bring the pro-life facts, such as are found in this book, to the attention of millions of people.

The names vary: Minnesota Citizens Concerned for Life, Women Concerned for the Unborn (Pittsburgh), Alliance for Life (Toronto), Society for the Protection of Unborn Children (England) ....of the Unborn Child (New Zealand), Americans United for Life (USA), Pro-Vita (Belgium), Laissez-les-Vivre (France), Nurses for Life, and hundreds of others.

Aren't these groups being formed only to fight permissive abortion laws?

Primarily they are educational, but flowing from the dissemination of this information has come increased opposition to the election of anti-life candidates and specific pressure for the passage of a Human Life Amendment.

Are they only concerned about abortion?

Definitely not. While this is their major thrust at present, they are concerned about the right of humans to live at any state of life, whether unborn or born. Infanticide, euthanasia, and other anti-life philosophies are also of great concern to such groups.

Almost all are "social activist" groups. As such they are primarily educational but can and do lobby for passage of bills relating to abortion and euthanasia.

Auxiliary non-profit foundations have been set up that are solely educational.

More recently, Right to Life Political Action Groups have been formed to support or oppose specific political candidates.

Are these groups doing anything to solve the social problems that might lead a woman to an abortion?

As organizations, such citizens groups limit their efforts to the educational and political area of abortion-infanticide-euthanasia. It is almost, however, the badge of membership of the concerned citizens who are its members to be active in working for many other social causes. Particularly those areas relating to adoption, defective and abused children and their care.

Aren't these organizations mostly front organizations for religious bodies?

Each city or area should have one major citizens group of a Right to Life type (by whatever name). This should not have affiliation with any religious group. Religious groups having similar goals should be warmly encouraged. They could work with or have laison with the central R.T.L. group but should not control it.

One such organization I know is against flouridation, sex education in school, birth control, sterilization, and abortion. Are you asking us to support groups like this?

You may if you wish, but your authors certainly would not work with them or support them in this multiplicity of efforts. All of the things you mentioned have their strong supporters and opponents, and each can and should be considered as an individual concern. Under no circumstances, however, should Right to Life groups diversify their efforts by supporting or opposing movements that do not directly relate to the value of every human life, such as abortion, euthanasia, or infanticide. If an organization dilutes its efforts as mentioned, it will find very few people who will support all of its goals, will probably find that the great majority of people will oppose them, and the group will end up being quite ineffective. Concentrate at this time on the unborn baby's right to life if you hope to be effective.

Hasn't the passage of pro-abortion laws and court decisions settled the issue?

Exactly the opposite has happened! In every county where abortion has become legal, there has developed an increasingly strong movement against abortion and primarily by such citizens groups.

In 1970, for instance, there were about 10 Right to Life groups in existence in the U.S.A. When the U.S. Supreme Court's Decision came in 1973, there were 300 groups. By 1978, over 2,000 U.S. cities had such groups and a national organization was beginning to coordinate their activity. Some have great influence. Your author's own city of Cincinnati (one million people) publishes a 4 page monthly newsletter with a distribution of over 75,000. (In the 1974 national elections, of 23 Representatives elected to Congress from Ohio, 17 were pledged to vote for a constitutional amendment to reverse the Supreme Court Decision).

What is the National U.S. Group?

There are a number of national groups. The only one that has delegate representation from every state is the National Right to Life Committee which is composed of the fifty state RTL organizations. These are made up of about 2000 local chapters. The NRLC's Washington office is at 419 7th St. N.W., Washington, D.C. 20004. (Phone 202-681-4396).

Its National Right to Life News is the best and most comprehensive source of current information that is available. If you don't get it you should. ($12.00 per year).

27

THE WORDS WE USE

"Reform" of abortion laws? Is the denial of the right of the unborn to live truly a "reform"? To use the word "reform" is to agree that laws protecting the unborn needed to be changed. It is important in this debate to consistently use words that accurately and incisively describe the truths of which we speak. Let's make words work for us, not against us. Let's remove the camouflage and show "repeal" or "updating" of abortion laws for what it is and speak of "permissive laws", "abolishment of all controls", "denial of the unborn child's right to life" or whatever is applicable.

It was George Orwell who pointed out that it is possible to distort language so that words take on the reverse·of their actual meaning. If words are taken from the language, it can also mean the removal of the concepts they epitomize from peoples' consciousness.

If there are two words that this applies to, they are "terminate" and "fetus." Remember each time you use either of these words today, you further the pro-abortion cause. To the average person, "terminate" does not mean the same as to kill, (but it is), and "fetus" definitely no longer falls on the listening ear as "human" but rather as "non-human glob." Every time you use the words fetus or terminate you advance the pro-abortion cause.

"Termination of pregnancy", "interruption of pregnancy", "retroactive contraception" are all verbal gymnastics behind which to hide. "Induced abortion" is more accurate. "Killing the life within the mother", "killing the fetus", or most to the point, "killing the unborn baby" directly face the issue, and therefore are the most honest and preferable terms to use.

"Product of conception", "fetal tissue", "glob of protoplasm", "feto-placental unit" and other high sounding phrases are all direct denials of the humanity of the growing child. Make up your mind. If you are convinced that this is a human life, call it such. Then consistently speak of "he" or "she", not "it", and speak of the "unborn", "pre-born", or "developing child" or "baby". It is easy to approve killing of a "fetus", much less so the killing of an "unborn baby".

"Medical murder" implies a judgment of the abortionist's knowledge of the humanity of the unborn child, and willful killing. This may not be true. We would suggest that the simple phrase of "killing" of the pre-born child cannot be challenged, is not judgmental, and directly states what is being done.

"Pre-natal euthanasia" is entirely accurate when describing killing of an unborn child because he is defective. Euthanasia (mercy killing) is killing an adult because he is or has become incompetent or defective. This can also apply to children in which case it is commonly called infanticide.

Do not accept the negative label of being "anti-abortion." Rather, always speak of this movement and philosophy as being "pro-life."

When referring to those who want abortion-on-demand, speak of "abortionists", of the "abortionist mentality", or of the "anti-life movement." Never accuse another person of not being sincere but do insist on accurate terms.

"Liberalized" abortion is also a misnomer. We see a liberal as a person very concerned about the rights and dignity of every other person in society. To be liberal is to kill? Let's quit using "liberalize" and say "permissive" or other more accurate terms.

"Freedom over her own body" is in fact freedom to kill another. Abortion, "a woman's right to choose" is really, a woman's right to kill. "Freedom of choice" is freedom to kill. If she is "pro-choice" she is "pro-choice to kill".

What if contraception has failed? If so she is pregnant. She is going to have a baby. She'll have the baby killed and delivered dead or she'll deliver a live baby but she'll have a baby.

How can we impose our values on the woman? Why should we allow her to impose her values on her defenseless baby, fatally?

Men have no right to speak about abortion? Its a woman's decision! Northerners had no right to speak about slavery? It was a slaveholder's decision!

Abortion Clinic? No, "Clinic" sounds like a place of curing and caring. That's a pro-abortion word. Rather use "abortion chamber," reminding us of gas chambers, for isn't one of every two humans who enters that place exterminated?

Fetal deformity? Do you call a born child deformed? No! Then why an unborn child? Call them all handicapped, a word that calls for love and help not revulsion.

Don't forget

Abortion kills babies

Euthanasia kills patients

28

WHAT TO DO?

1) Pray

As if this were the only thing that matters, for in truth perhaps it is. Pray that God would allow our people to come to their senses (and to their knees) before we destroy ourselves.

2) Educate

Yourself and others. Read and re-read this book. Have your family read it and then lend it to six other people. It'll get lost, so get another and start again. Speak to others, discuss, give other literature.

3) Work

For the service groups (Birthright), the educational groups (Right to Life), the political groups (Political Action Committee). Work in any and all of the ways needed, for the unborn, the aged, the unfortunate. It is only through the continuing gift of our love in helping others that we will win over those who have turned to the violence of utilitarian killing to seek their ends.

4) Contribute

Time and effort and money to this effort. The pro-life effort is characterized by the heroic efforts of it's volunteers and by the fact that none of the groups ever have any money, they merely exist from less debt to more debt.

Your stewardship is needed.

5) Vote

In the primary and in the general elections. It will be through this process that the wish of the people will be translated into electing representatives whose convictions are either pro-life or anti-life. It will only be through this process that laws and constitutional amendments can be passed that will again protect and value all human life.

6) Write

Letters, write letters, write letters. Mark off each Tuesday on your kitchen calendar. After you've written that week's letter, cross it off. Do this and keep doing it until the Human Life Amendment passes or you reverse your nation's pro-abortion laws.

Who to? To your National Legislators (in the U.S. to your Senators and Representatives); to your state or provincial legislators (in the U.S., your state Senator & Representative); to your newspapers, your local and national TV and radio stations; to sponsors of programs; to your local government, health department, etc.; then start the cycle again.

Keep them brief, courteous, pointed, and by all means, sign your name. Keep writing.

God Bless You,

Barbara and Jack Willke

RESOURCES

See illustrated back pages for most widely used materials, in addition we recommend

ABORTION, AS IT IS by Dr. & Mrs. Willke, Hayes Pub. Co. $75.00 their newly revised most effective audio-visual, see ad p. 205.

NEW PERSPECTIVES ON HUMAN ABORTION by Hilgers, Horan & Mall, 500 pp $12.00, University Pub. of America. A new comprehensive in-depth updating on the issue.

A PRIVATE CHOICE by John Noonan, Life Cycle Books, $4.95. The most detailed treatment to date of the social and legal history of abortion in the U.S.

ABORTION IN PERSPECTIVE, by D. DeMarco, Hayes Pub. Co., Inc., $4.95. A fascinating exploration of many facets of the abortion problem from a gifted philosopher, written for the average reader. Some really new insights.

ABORTION, THE BIBLE AND THE CHRISTIAN. Dr. D. Shoemaker, Hayes Pub. Co. What the Bible says about abortion (see ad p. 210).

THE GERMAN EUTHANASIA PROGRAM. Dr. F. Wertham, Hayes Pub. Co. The program that preceded the Holocaust (see ad p. 208).

AUDIO-VISUALS, Right to Life of Greater Cincinnati, Inc., P.O. Box 24073, Cincinnati, Ohio 45224. Film of a suction abortion, $85.00; convention-size laminated exhibit, $350.00; sets of 5 x 7 color pictures, $14.00; and audio cassette of heartbeat of 8 week unborn, $2.00.

MEDICAL HOLOCAUSTS, 2 Vol. by Wm. Brennan, $8.95 per volume, Nordland Pub. Inc. Exterminative medicine in Nazi Germany and America.

ABORTING AMERICA, by Bernard Nathanson, M.D. The man who "presided over 65,000 deaths" writes of his change and present pro-life conviction. $3.95 paper. Life Cycle Books.

DEATH, DYING & EUTHANASIA by Horan & Mall, 800 pg., University Pub. the best book yet on the right-to-die issue, $10.00.

POPULATION GROWTH, Colin Clark, $2.00 LIFE, 900 N. Broadway, Suite 725, Santa Ana, California 92701. An impressive short work. It takes **Population Bomb** and cuts it to shreds exposing its fallacies with knifelike precision.

RIGHT TO LIVE, RIGHT TO DIE, Koop, $2.50, Life Cycle Books, by the famous Pediatric Surgeon, on Infanticide, Abortion and Euthanasia.

CANADA

For faster delivery, almost all of the materials recommended here are available from:

LIFE CYCLE BOOKS
2205 Danforth Ave.
Toronto, Ontario
Canada M4C 1K4
(416) 690-5860

ABORTION, AS IT IS

BY DR. AND MRS. WILLKE

The answer to the educational needs of the pro-life movement. A simple, beyond refutation, and flexible presentation. With this program, any pro-life speaker becomes startlingly effective.

TWO CASSETTES, 4 Sides, 122 Slides in Kodak Carrousel Tray $75.00
Same without tray $70.00

the Court decision — fetal development — definition of human life — civil rights issue — Discrimination on basis of race, color, age, handicap, place of residence — choice — wanted — population — rape — war and capital punishment — mini abortions — surgical and drug abortions — euthanasia — Court rulings in Roe and later decisions — their effects — the human life amendment(s) — effect needed — effects of birth control — & much, much more

audible beeps, electronic signals

Library Pack

To balance the everpresent pro-abortion books on the shelves. Selected by the Nat. RTL Education Committee.

— Handbook on Abortion
— Abortion & Social Justice
— German Euthanasia Program
— The Right to Live, Right to Die
— Abortion in Perspective
— Handbook on Population

} all six hardbound $30.00

— Population Growth
— Death Without Dignity
— Care of the Dying
— Handbook on Abortion (Spanish)
— Abortion, Bible & Christian

} may be added $20.00

WALL POSTERS
24" x 36"

COPIES
one $2.00
10 .... $1.50
100 .... $1.10

WHO IMPOSED their morality on these little people?

COLOR   BLACK & WHITE

HOW BABIES GROW

● For pre-school to adolescent
● A sensitive telling of the beautiful story of conception to birth. 10 min., 18 slides
● 10 min., 18 slides, audible & electronic beeps

$17.95

Pro Life Materials by Dr. & Mrs. Willke

Available in
English
Spanish
French
German
Italian
Portuguese
Dutch
Norwegian
Hungarian
Polish
Japanese
Chinese
Swedish
Turkish

The Brochure that reversed opinion in Michigan to a pro-life majority in their referendum.

Full color for mass distribution.

100 copies	....	12¢ each
1,000 copies	....	9¢ each
10,000 copies	....	7.5¢ each

Supreme Court brochure, available in English language only, to be used after they have seen LIFE OR DEATH.
Full color for mass distribution.

Brief, hard hitting facts on development in the womb.

Envelope size.

Easy to include with every letter, bill, or mailing you send.

Pass out at a sports event, a fair, or a convention, at an abortion clinic.

AN ENVELOPE STUFFER —A MINI BROCHURE *in English, Spanish, French, German, Italian, Portuguese, Croation, Swedish.*

100 copies	.....	4¢ each plus post.
1,000 copies	.....	3¢ each plus post.
10,000 copies	.....	2.5¢ each plus post.
100,000 copies	.....	2.0¢ each plus post.

208

Pro Life Materials by Dr. & Mrs. Willke

A live recording of a dialogue between Dr. and Mrs. Willke and 500 college students. The question? If an enduring marriage is your goal would some experience in intimate sex before marriage be wise?

Considering only medical and psychosocial aspects they establish rapport, discuss, explain and analyze, finally, with the students, concluding that for most, it is smart to wait.

Cassettes   4 sides with manual $14.95

SEX & LOVE
explores the dating years

MARRIAGE
a short pre-marriage course

$2.95 $2.95

$1.50
16th Printing

For Parents

"I greatly admire your splendid work. It warms my heart to read your fine, sensible, reverent and manly work."
REV. NORMAN VINCENT PEALE

"A top guide for sex education."
THE PARENT EDUCATOR

. . . *"If you want a book on sex education that tells you what to say, when and how, you can find no better in America today . . . this little gem outstrips them all."*
THE COLUMBUS TIMES

For Parents and Teachers

NEW

*the answer to
Sex Education in School*

FINALLY READ

**a reasonable
middle of the road
answer**

**this carefully
before you do
anything in
your school**

In simple, direct fashion, Dr. & Mrs. Willke have again distilled their years of study, lecturing, traveling, and consulting throughout the U.S. and Canada on the subject of sex education in school.

$4.95

**FOR
All School Officials
All Teachers
All Parents**

Rev. Shoemaker has brought together the relevant Bible passages and explained them in sensitive, reverent and simple fashion.

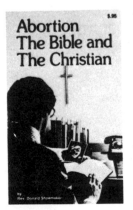

Single copy . . . . @ $1.25 ea.
10 or more copies . . . @ $1.00 ea.
100 or more copies . . . @ $ .88 ea.

"This booklet presents the Biblical viewpoint. I find this to be a very useful work and would recommend it."

*Jack Cottrell, Ph.D.
Professor of Theology
and Ethics
Cincinnati Christian
Seminary*

"I find nothing in Mr. Shoemaker's manuscript that would be contrary to Catholic teaching on the subject."

*Rev. Eugene H. Maly
Prof. of Sacred
Scripture
Mt. St. Mary's
Seminary
Norwood, Ohio*